Today, Crac des Chevaliers is a beautiful fortress that you can visit as a tourist. If the howling wind drops for a moment, listen hard. You might just hear the ghostly echo of horses' hooves on the cobbles, and orders shouted in medieval French!

Many castles elsewhere in the world are older or bigger than Crac des Chevaliers. Modern castles are much stronger. But none has aroused more fear, anger, and envy. No wonder an Arab writer called it "a bone in the throat of the Muslims."

The castle was a stronghold of the European Christians who ruled the Holy Land for nearly two centuries. Its warrior monks divided their time between battle and prayer. Their defense of the castle is an exciting story of faith, blood, and glory.

On a windswept hilltop in Syria stands one of the world's mightiest and most amazing castles—Crac des Chevaliers. Despite earthquakes, torrential rains, and scorching heat, its 900-year old walls and beautifully carved arches still stand firm.

experience

CASTLE

written by
RICHARD PLATT

CASTLES AND KNIGHTS

CASTLES IN HISTORY

Towering high above the land around, the solid walls of castles are impressive reminders of power and wealth from the past. For castles were once the massive (and costly) stone strongholds of proud rulers, and bases for the warriors at their command.

First castles

Fortresses and protected camps have a long history—they were first built in Mesopotamia (now Iraq) more than 5,000 years ago. The most famous European castles date from the Middle Ages (roughly the 5th to the 16th centuries). From the safety of their walls, lords and monarchs controlled their lands with help from armies of knights. These horseback warriors rode into battle dressed in iron armor. Their swords and long lances made them dangerous and frightening foes. At first knights fought out of duty. In exchange for their service on the battlefield, they received lands and homes from their more powerful masters.

Castle armies

Knights were the glittering, colorful officers of much larger armies. These also included many humbler soldiers who fought on foot. Known as infantry, they owed a debt of duty to their knight masters—just as the knights served more powerful lords. In time, though, debts of duty changed to money payments. Then gold, not promises, guaranteed a battlefield lined with armored warriors and archers.

> "They cruelly oppressed the wretched men of the land with castle-works; and when the castles were made, they filled them with devils and evil men."
>
> *The Anglo-Saxon Chronicle, 1137*

In peacetime, castles hosted great banquets, like this one in 15th-century France. Guests judged their host's wealth by the number of dishes served and the rarity of the ingredients.

Chaotic lands

With their masters and foot soldiers, knights fought to control a restless world. For in the Middle Ages Europe was not divided up into large, peaceful countries with neat borders as it is today. Monarchs struggled to keep hold of power in lands that were often torn apart by violent and chaotic feuds. They could rule over large regions only by making alliances with other powerful people. Each of these lords controlled a small area—and castles played a vital part in their schemes.

Built to last

Designed from the ground up for defense, castles used ingenious plans and clever features to keep attackers out. Solid foundations discouraged undermining (tunneling into the castle). The height of the walls aimed to protect them from attackers on ladders. Their thickness helped them resist stone missiles thrown from giant catapults. The weakest points, the gates, were defended with cunning and murderous traps.

Through jousting—mock charges with lances—knights kept their fighting skills sharp. In this 13th-century illustration, the king of Sicily defeats his rival.

Castles relied on manor farms, like this one outside the castle walls, to provide the food they needed for the soldiers inside. Sale of farm produce also provided income for castles.

What castles were for

As strongholds, castles provided their owners with safe homes in unsafe times. However, they were much more than houses with thick walls. The most important job of a castle was to control a region—to protect it from attack and conquest by a warlike neighbor. So castles were built at carefully chosen places. They guarded river crossings such as bridges and fords. They loomed above important roads or near passes in high mountain ranges. Or they clung to hard-to-reach (but strategic) hilltops.

Castle supplies

War wasn't the only reason for a castle's position, though. A castle garrison (guard force) needed food and drink to survive attack. So a castle site had a deep well, a spring, or a river that provided water for the troops and their animals. Food supplies came from the farms that surrounded most castles. Cool, dark rooms within the castle walls were warehouses for surplus crops. These stores could feed the garrison in a long siege (an encircling attack that cut off supplies from outside).

Luxurious home

Though military might was a castle's main purpose, it was usually also a home—and sometimes a luxurious one. Many had grand halls where the owner might entertain important guests, with great kitchens and wine cellars to match. Living rooms and bedrooms, heated by roaring fires and hung with tapestries, provided the castle's owner and his family with privacy that few others enjoyed.

Building a better castle

No two medieval castles are exactly alike, because ideas about warfare and defense changed all the time. The masons who constructed castles aimed to make each one better and stronger than those that had gone before. Their employers exchanged ideas for new defenses and copied the best features from their enemies' castles. Wars in distant lands introduced castle builders to new defensive architecture. And some of the most radical ideas about castle defenses came from the most distant wars of all—the crusades in the Holy Land.

Building a castle on a towering crag, like this one on the Var River in France, made it easy to defend—but almost impossible to supply with food during a siege.

Through these holes atop the walls, the castle guard dropped rocks on attackers below. European masons probably copied the idea from Muslim castles.

When England's King Edward I began building Harlech Castle in Wales in 1283, he included in it design features he had seen on castles in the Holy Land 12 years earlier.

THE BATTLEGROUND

In the most destructive wars of the Middle Ages, Christians and Muslims struggled for control of the lands to the east of the Mediterranean Sea, where Lebanon, Syria, Israel, and Palestine are today. To Christians, this was the Holy Land because Jesus Christ had lived and died here. But by the 11th century much of the Holy Land was ruled by Muslims. This led the kingdoms of Europe to send knights to protect the Christian shrines they believed were threatened. The religious wars they fought were called crusades. Brutal and bloody, the crusades divided Christians and Muslims with a bitter rivalry that has never been forgotten.

AMERICA
ASIA
EUROPE
AFRICA

N

CYPRUS

Since the time of Jesus, Christian **pilgrims** had been visiting holy sites in Palestine. The conquest of the region by Muslim Arabs in the 7th century made these religious journeys, called pilgrimages, more difficult and dangerous.

Just 100 miles (150 km) from the coast of the Holy Land, Cyprus was in a strategic location. English king Richard I captured the island in 1191. It became a major stronghold for the crusades, and a supply base secure from Muslim attack.

Though some **crusaders** marched to the Holy Land, many traveled by sea. Once Christians captured the port of Tyre in 1124, Egyptian Muslim sailors had nowhere on the coast to get fresh water. This limited the range of their war fleet, making the Mediterranean safer for Christian shipping.

THREE FAITHS

For Jews, the land at the Mediterranean's eastern end was a homeland, but they had been persecuted and driven from it since Roman times. Christians also claimed it as their own, because it was where the stories of the Bible took place. Muslims, too, believed they had a right to Jerusalem, the place from which they believed the Prophet Muhammad rose to heaven.

THE STAR OF DAVID, SYMBOL OF THE JEWISH FAITH

A CERAMIC DECORATED WITH MUSLIM HOLY WORDS

A CRUSADER TOMBSTONE AT TYRE

---

pilgrims People who journey to a sacred place to pray and to show their religious faith.

crusaders Men who answered the church's call to fight in the Holy Land in return for the forgiveness of their sins.

crusader states The new Christian states, such as the Kingdom of Jerusalem, set up by the crusaders in the Holy Land.

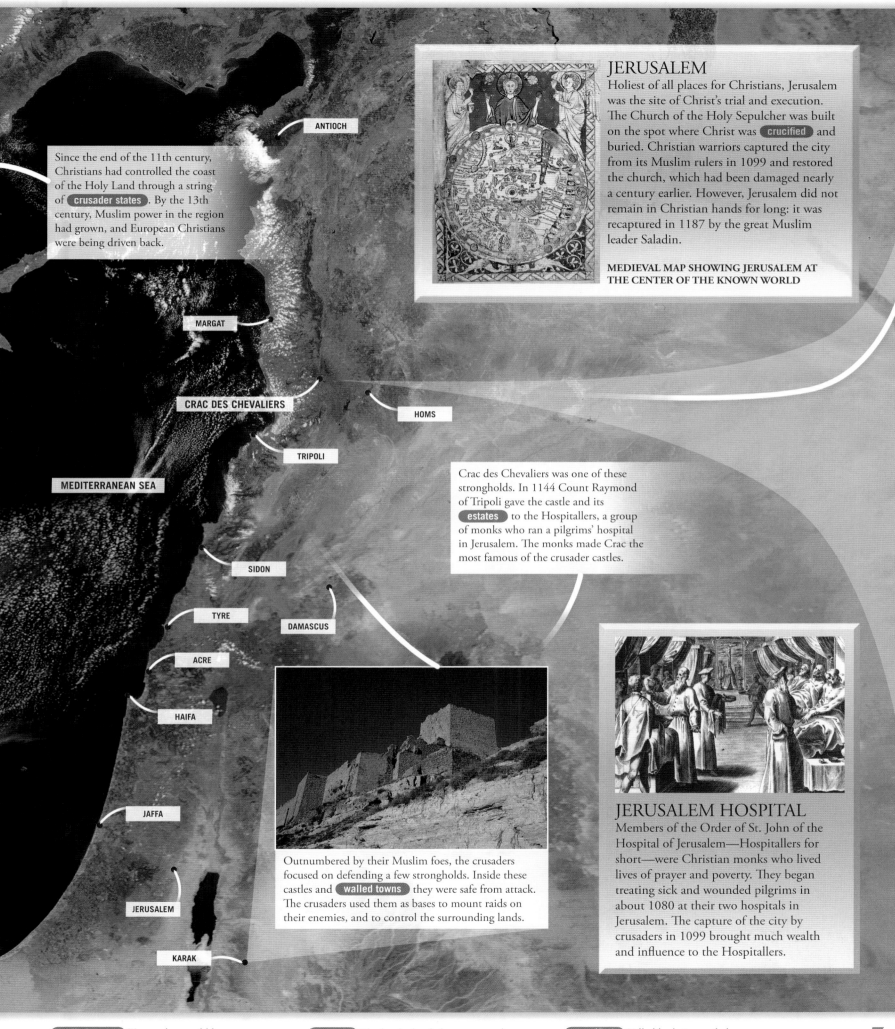

ANTIOCH

JERUSALEM
Holiest of all places for Christians, Jerusalem was the site of Christ's trial and execution. The Church of the Holy Sepulcher was built on the spot where Christ was crucified and buried. Christian warriors captured the city from its Muslim rulers in 1099 and restored the church, which had been damaged nearly a century earlier. However, Jerusalem did not remain in Christian hands for long: it was recaptured in 1187 by the great Muslim leader Saladin.

MEDIEVAL MAP SHOWING JERUSALEM AT THE CENTER OF THE KNOWN WORLD

Since the end of the 11th century, Christians had controlled the coast of the Holy Land through a string of crusader states. By the 13th century, Muslim power in the region had grown, and European Christians were being driven back.

MARGAT

CRAC DES CHEVALIERS

HOMS

TRIPOLI

MEDITERRANEAN SEA

Crac des Chevaliers was one of these strongholds. In 1144 Count Raymond of Tripoli gave the castle and its estates to the Hospitallers, a group of monks who ran a pilgrims' hospital in Jerusalem. The monks made Crac the most famous of the crusader castles.

SIDON

TYRE

DAMASCUS

ACRE

HAIFA

JAFFA

Outnumbered by their Muslim foes, the crusaders focused on defending a few strongholds. Inside these castles and walled towns they were safe from attack. The crusaders used them as bases to mount raids on their enemies, and to control the surrounding lands.

JERUSALEM

KARAK

JERUSALEM HOSPITAL
Members of the Order of St. John of the Hospital of Jerusalem—Hospitallers for short—were Christian monks who lived lives of prayer and poverty. They began treating sick and wounded pilgrims in about 1080 at their two hospitals in Jerusalem. The capture of the city by crusaders in 1099 brought much wealth and influence to the Hospitallers.

---

walled towns Towns that could be defended against attacking armies. Many ancient towns had defensive walls.

estates The lands that belong to a castle and that supply it with income and food.

crucified Killed by being nailed to a wooden cross. This was a common form of execution in Roman times.

CRAC'S CRUCIAL POSITION

In the region surrounding Crac, the Hospitallers have their own ministate. They are already important in the Holy Land through their hospital work in Jerusalem and elsewhere, but by the middle of the 12th century, caring for the sick and wounded is no longer their only mission. They also have a military purpose, fighting as the **shock troops** in crusader battles. The gift of the castle means that the Hospitallers have a military base. Its position makes it immensely valuable. They have strengthened it to protect the eastern frontier of the Christian domain, and it has become a center for the administration of their little state.

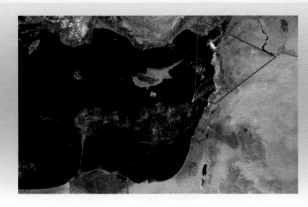

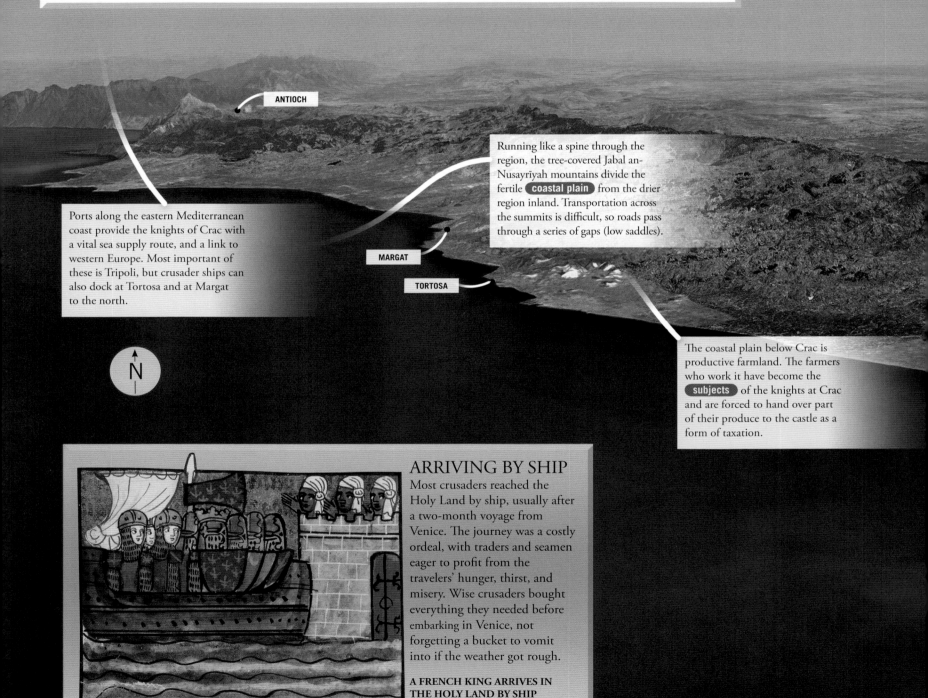

ANTIOCH

MARGAT

TORTOSA

Ports along the eastern Mediterranean coast provide the knights of Crac with a vital sea supply route, and a link to western Europe. Most important of these is Tripoli, but crusader ships can also dock at Tortosa and at Margat to the north.

Running like a spine through the region, the tree-covered Jabal an-Nusayriyah mountains divide the fertile **coastal plain** from the drier region inland. Transportation across the summits is difficult, so roads pass through a series of gaps (low saddles).

The coastal plain below Crac is productive farmland. The farmers who work it have become the **subjects** of the knights at Crac and are forced to hand over part of their produce to the castle as a form of taxation.

N

ARRIVING BY SHIP

Most crusaders reached the Holy Land by ship, usually after a two-month voyage from Venice. The journey was a costly ordeal, with traders and seamen eager to profit from the travelers' hunger, thirst, and misery. Wise crusaders bought everything they needed before embarking in Venice, not forgetting a bucket to vomit into if the weather got rough.

A FRENCH KING ARRIVES IN THE HOLY LAND BY SHIP

shock troops Soldiers specially trained and equipped to carry out an assault.

coastal plain A flat area of land in between the sea and higher ground where the Earth's crust folds into mountain ranges.

subjects People who are under the power of a ruler.

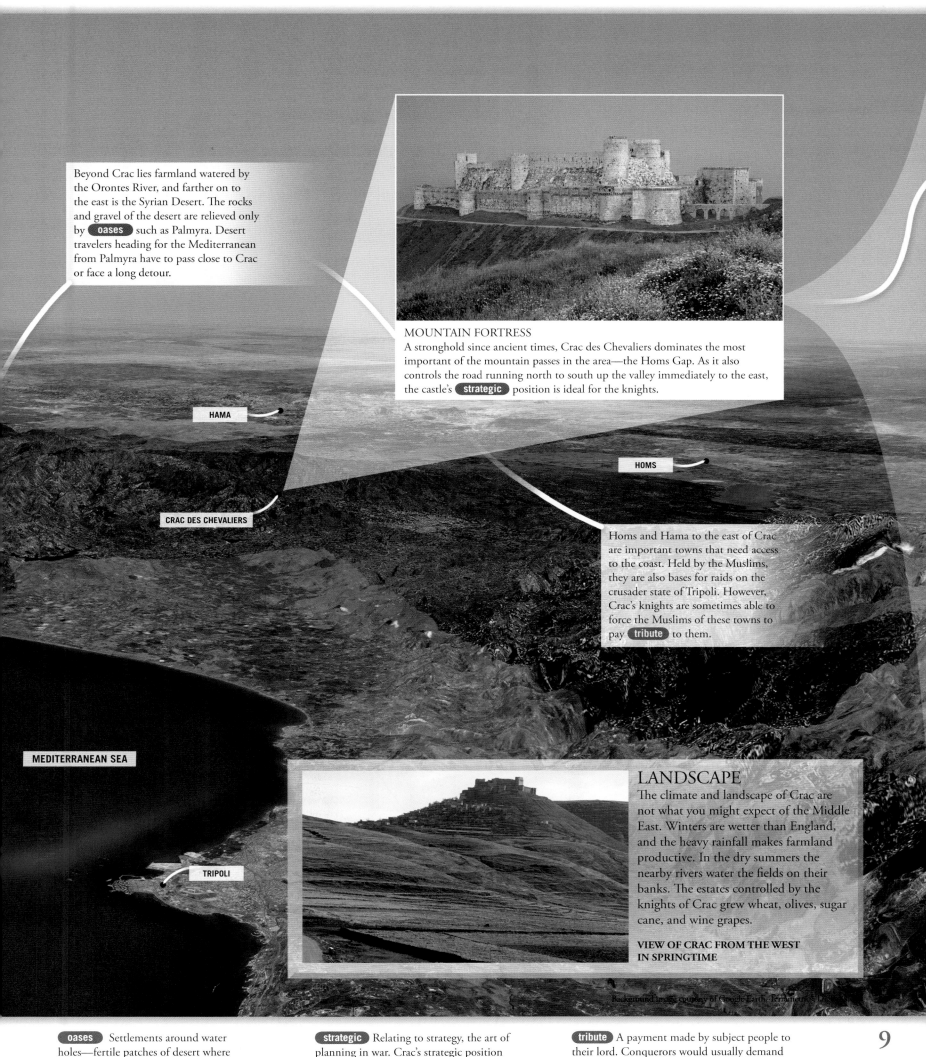

Beyond Crac lies farmland watered by the Orontes River, and farther on to the east is the Syrian Desert. The rocks and gravel of the desert are relieved only by oases such as Palmyra. Desert travelers heading for the Mediterranean from Palmyra have to pass close to Crac or face a long detour.

HAMA

HOMS

CRAC DES CHEVALIERS

MEDITERRANEAN SEA

TRIPOLI

MOUNTAIN FORTRESS
A stronghold since ancient times, Crac des Chevaliers dominates the most important of the mountain passes in the area—the Homs Gap. As it also controls the road running north to south up the valley immediately to the east, the castle's strategic position is ideal for the knights.

Homs and Hama to the east of Crac are important towns that need access to the coast. Held by the Muslims, they are also bases for raids on the crusader state of Tripoli. However, Crac's knights are sometimes able to force the Muslims of these towns to pay tribute to them.

LANDSCAPE
The climate and landscape of Crac are not what you might expect of the Middle East. Winters are wetter than England, and the heavy rainfall makes farmland productive. In the dry summers the nearby rivers water the fields on their banks. The estates controlled by the knights of Crac grew wheat, olives, sugar cane, and wine grapes.

VIEW OF CRAC FROM THE WEST IN SPRINGTIME

Background image courtesy of Google Earth, Terrametrics

---

oases Settlements around water holes—fertile patches of desert where groundwater reaches the surface.

strategic Relating to strategy, the art of planning in war. Crac's strategic position gave it a military advantage.

tribute A payment made by subject people to their lord. Conquerors would usually demand tribute from those conquered.

HOW CRAC DES CHEVALIERS GREW

The castle given to the Hospitallers was known as the castle of the Kurds, because it had once been guarded by Kurdish soldiers. The Hospitallers saw that the castle's position made it strong, and they set to work to make sure it could withstand attack from any direction. In two main phases of building, they created an inner ring of walls and towers, then surrounded this with an outer wall. The result was one of the finest medieval castles anywhere in the Christian world. From this hilltop they could control vast areas of surrounding countryside. Even if threatened, they could return to the safety of the place that became known simply as Crac des Chevaliers—Castle of the Knights.

1142

Since all signs of it have disappeared, we can only guess at the size of the castle that the Hospitallers inherited. It may have been a simple stone wall enclosing the summit on which the present castle stands.

Little remains of the defenses that once protected the south side. Probably built in the first **Frankish** period of construction, they may have been just a series of ditches or wooden walls aimed at stopping invaders from bringing **siege engines** too close.

1169

The knights probably began rebuilding Crac as soon as they took over. By 1169 they had completed a ring of strong walls, reinforced by square towers. This enclosure hid a chapel, **vaulted** rooms, and possibly a hall. Over the next half century earthquakes twice damaged Crac. In the repairs that followed, the knights added first an outer ring of walls, then extra defenses to the tops of the walls (main picture).

Even today, different phases of construction are plain to see in the walls of Crac. The southeast corner, probably among the last of the Hospitallers' construction projects, is made of badly fitting rubble blocks. The carved stonework on top is a recent restoration.

vaulted A structure with a roof or ceiling that is arched. The stone-vaulted roof was a medieval invention unknown to the Romans.

Frankish The name given by medieval Muslims to anything western European.

siege engines Heavy wooden constructions used to attack a castle by battering its defenses or scaling its walls.

-N→

In the 1230s the knights added an arched **cloister** to their great hall in Crac's main courtyard. Its decorative stonework is as fine as that found in the cathedrals of Europe. The cloister reminded visitors that the knights belonged to a wealthy monastic order.

Crac had always had a back door—a **postern** gate in the north wall. In the final phase of building, after 1250, the knights built extra towers on either side of the postern in the outer wall, and strengthened the tall northwest tower where a second postern pierced the inner wall.

The Hospitallers were wealthy in the early 13th century and spent lavishly on building the outer enclosing walls. Rising to an imposing 30 ft (9 m) in places, they are strengthened with six major towers and several smaller ones. However, after 1250 the money ran out so new building work was limited.

After 1250 the knights strengthened the entrance, making the approach to Crac more elaborate. Leading into the courtyard was a gatehouse that would not be out of place in any castle of the period. But to reach its fortified doorway, an attacker had to climb a zigzag slope under fire from the castle.

Beyond the walls of Crac clustered the burgus—a suburb. Long since destroyed, it may have been a mix of houses belonging to the knights' local allies, craft workshops, offices squeezed out of the castle's cramped interior, and extra stabling for the knights' many horses.

BUILDERS

Castles like Crac employed huge numbers of laborers and skilled **masons**. At Harlech Castle (see page 5), which was a similar size to Crac, 227 masons cut stone on the site. They were supplied with the stone by 115 quarriers. At Crac, the master mason who controlled a crew of similar size would have come from France, where he might have learned his trade building cathedrals. Laborers would have been recruited locally—by force if necessary.

MEDIEVAL WORKERS WITH THEIR TOOLS

cloister A covered walkway usually around a square, having open arches on the inside and a wall on the outside.

masons People skilled at building with stone. Medieval masons were important people.

postern A small back door or gate, especially one for private use.

11

THE CRUSADES

KILLING FOR GOD

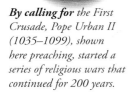

By calling for the First Crusade, Pope Urban II (1035–1099), shown here preaching, started a series of religious wars that continued for 200 years.

Christian crosses stitched onto their clothes earned the crusaders their name: "crusaders" means "the crossed ones" or "those who have taken the cross."

With a cry of "God wills it!" Christians from all over medieval Europe gave up their families and their livelihoods to go and fight in a distant land. They knew they might never return home. But burning religious faith—and the promise of a fast-track to heaven—inspired them to "take the cross" and fight in the crusades. These religious wars aimed to reclaim the Holy Land from the Muslims who lived there.

The pope's call to arms

The crusades began with the preaching of Urban II, the pope (holy leader) of the Catholic Church. In the spring of 1095 he toured France, speaking to huge meetings. He told of the sufferings of pilgrims in the Holy Land. He warned of the threat to Christians in the east from the Seljuqs—Muslim Turks from central Asia. And he reminded the crowds that Muslims had destroyed Jerusalem's most holy church less than a century earlier. The pope ended his sermon by calling for a holy war, a crusade to recapture Jerusalem.

Rapid reaction force

The crowds' reaction to the pope's sermons was far better than he expected. Within a few months, a ragged and disorganized army of poor but devout Christians had gathered. They had stitched crosses to their clothes and were heading for the Holy Land. The following year wealthy and well-armed Christian knights from all over Europe followed them. By 1097 the crusaders had encircled the ancient city of Antioch.

Sieges and success

After an exhausting and desperate siege, Antioch fell to the crusaders in June 1098. A year later so, too, did Jerusalem. In both cities, the crusaders slaughtered every Muslim and Jew they found until the buildings were full of corpses and the streets running with blood. Today, these massacres of innocent people seem cruel and barbaric. But to the crusaders they were vital. They believed their victims were "godless" heathens. Killing them was a religious duty. The murders provoked in Muslims a bitter hatred for the crusaders.

> "Let this one cry be raised by all the soldiers of God: It is the will of God!"
>
> *Robert the Monk, reporting on Urban II's sermon at Clermont, 1095*

Crusaders made the sea journey to the Holy Land in stinking galleys (rowed ships) like these. All but the wealthiest passengers slept head-to-foot on deck.

The first crusader armies *marched overland from Europe, covering as much as 2,500 miles (4,000 km). Ships carried most later crusaders, making the journey quicker, though hardly much safer.*

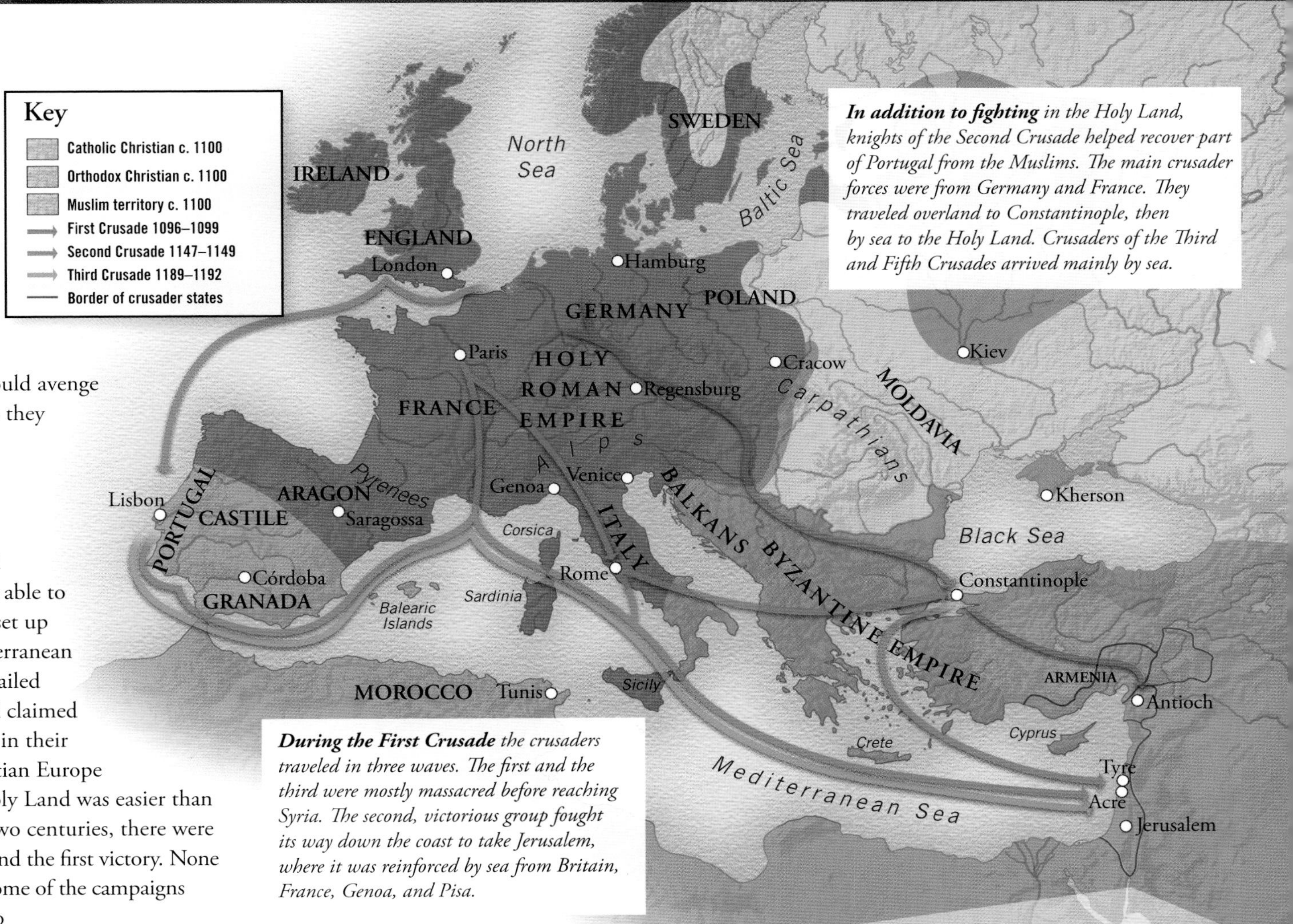

Key

- Catholic Christian c. 1100
- Orthodox Christian c. 1100
- Muslim territory c. 1100
- → First Crusade 1096–1099
- → Second Crusade 1147–1149
- → Third Crusade 1189–1192
- — Border of crusader states

In addition to fighting *in the Holy Land, knights of the Second Crusade helped recover part of Portugal from the Muslims. The main crusader forces were from Germany and France. They traveled overland to Constantinople, then by sea to the Holy Land. Crusaders of the Third and Fifth Crusades arrived mainly by sea.*

(Map labels: North Sea, SWEDEN, IRELAND, ENGLAND, London, Hamburg, Baltic Sea, Paris, GERMANY, POLAND, Cracow, Kiev, HOLY ROMAN EMPIRE, Regensburg, Carpathians, MOLDAVIA, FRANCE, Alps, Venice, Genoa, Kherson, ARAGON, Pyrenees, ITALY, Corsica, Black Sea, PORTUGAL, CASTILE, Saragossa, Rome, BALKANS, BYZANTINE EMPIRE, Constantinople, Lisbon, Córdoba, Sardinia, GRANADA, Balearic Islands, ARMENIA, MOROCCO, Tunis, Sicily, Crete, Cyprus, Antioch, Mediterranean Sea, Tyre, Acre, Jerusalem)

Two centuries later they would avenge the Antioch massacre when they recaptured the city.

Crusader kingdoms

The First Crusade was a spectacular and unexpected success. The crusaders were able to push back the Seljuqs and set up kingdoms along the Mediterranean shore. Devout Christians hailed the victory as a miracle and claimed that God had helped them in their campaign. However, Christian Europe found that winning the Holy Land was easier than keeping it. Over the next two centuries, there were many more crusades to defend the first victory. None had the same success, and some of the campaigns were disasters. In addition to being slaughtered in bitter battles, crusaders died of hunger and disease.

Saladin's revenge

A turning point came in 1187 when the sultan (ruler) of Egypt and Syria, Saladin (1137–1193), recaptured Jerusalem. The Third Crusade to recover the city was only a partial victory, and Christians would never again rule Jerusalem for longer than 10 years. The crusader kingdoms held out for longer. Saladin's attacks had reduced them to three small regions around Antioch, Tripoli, and north of Acre. However, by 1197 the crusaders had recovered most of the coast. For the next 50 years or so Christians thrived in the Holy Land and even traded peacefully with their Muslim neighbors.

During the First Crusade *the crusaders traveled in three waves. The first and the third were mostly massacred before reaching Syria. The second, victorious group fought its way down the coast to take Jerusalem, where it was reinforced by sea from Britain, France, Genoa, and Pisa.*

> "Piles of heads, hands, and feet were to be seen in the streets of the city. It was necessary to pick one's way over the bodies of men and horses... Indeed, it was a just and splendid judgment of God..."

Raymond d'Aguilliers describes the capture of Jerusalem in his History of the Franks

Baybars

But then, a new threat grew in Egypt. The Mamluks, once a class of Turkish-born warrior-slaves, had seized power there. By 1260, they had won control of all the land around the crusader kingdoms. Year by year, they raided and captured more and more of the Christian lands. Under the command of Sultan Baybars I, the Mamluks became more ambitious. They saw a chance to drive the hated Westerners out of the Holy Land for good. By 1268, Baybars had captured Caesarea, Arsur, Saphet, and Antioch. Though the crusader states were fatally weakened and isolated, some Christian strongholds still defied the Muslim onslaught. The mightiest of these was Crac des Chevaliers.

The crusaders established *small kingdoms along the coast of the Holy Land, naming them after the cities at their hearts. The European settlers lived in these cities and in walled towns. Outside, local Christians still formed the majority of the population in many parts of the region.*

THE CHAPEL

The center of life in Crac des Chevaliers is the chapel, for in many ways the whole castle is a fortified monastery. The "brother knights" who live, work, and train here are monks first, and soldiers second. Their daily routine revolves around a regular timetable of prayer and religious ritual within the chapel's walls. Each day in the early morning most of the brother knights file into the chapel to celebrate Mass—the most important service of their Catholic religion. So when a messenger reaches Crac bringing news of danger it is natural that he heads straight for the place where most of the brothers are assembled.

When not praying on their knees, the brother knights sit on hard benches. A monk's life was not supposed to be easy. The Hospitallers' second Master, Raymond de Puy, set rules for the order that demanded "...poverty (having few possessions), chastity (purity), and obedience."

Standing at the northeast corner of the inner stronghold, Crac's chapel was probably built in about 1170 following an earthquake. Its solid construction ensures that later tremors would do no further damage. The chapel's priest leads the service from the altar at the northeast end.

As the most sacred and precious part of the castle, the chapel is beautifully decorated with religious scenes. A Syrian Christian artist has painted the pictures over plaster covering the arched north walls. Some fragments of his work survive there today.

Crac's brothers follow the same timetable of prayer, called the hours, as other monks. It begins with Matins at midnight. Prime follows at 6 a.m., with **Mass** at 9 a.m. and 11 a.m. In the afternoon and evening there are three more services: Nones, Vespers, and Compline. Each lasts 30–60 minutes.

CRUSADING MONASTIC ORDERS

The idea of warrior monks might seem surprising today, but it was not odd in the Middle Ages. Christians believed that their religion was under attack, and warfare was the natural way for **devout** people to defend it. The first of the crusading monks were the Knights Templar. Their **order** was set up in 1118 to protect pilgrims after the First Crusade. Their rivals, the Hospitallers, became fighting monks some 40 years later. Both orders grew rich on gifts of money and land in Europe, which supported their work in the Holy land.

SIMON DE MONTFORT, AN ENGLISH TEMPLAR, WITH A SHIELD DISPLAYING THE CRUSADER CROSS

Mass The most important service of the day, in which Christ's Last Supper is remembered by sharing bread and wine.

order A society of people who have taken holy vows so that they can devote themselves to a religious cause.

devout Deeply religious. Joining the crusades was one of the highest expressions of faith during the Middle Ages.

THE HOSPITALLERS

The order of the Hospital of St. John was the most successful, and most famous, of the crusading monastic orders. Their work caring for the sick and fighting for Christianity made them immensely wealthy and powerful, and they obeyed nobody except the pope—the head of the Catholic church.

POPE PASCAL II BLESSES THE HOSPITALLERS' RULES IN 1113

Morning sunbeams light the painted walls of the chapel. The window in the northeast wall is small, but afternoon sunlight floods through the window at the other end. The windows are just openings—there is no glass to keep out the cold winter's winds.

Setting parts of the service to music makes it easier to remember. The chapel walls echo to the sound of **plainsong**. However, the monks may have accompanied the singing on a shawm, an instrument similar to a modern bassoon.

Knights normally wear on their heads large skull-caps, turbans, or wide-brimmed hats. At prayer they take these off, but they keep on their **coifs** that they wear underneath. All the knights wear **habits**. The wearing of mail coats and other armor is banned in the chapel.

plainsong Holy verses sung in unison and without a musical accompaniment. Plainsong is a medieval monastic tradition.

coifs Small white caps worn beneath another hat. Coifs were also worn beneath mail coats.

habits Coarse, loose-fitting robes worn by monks, as befitted people who had taken a vow of poverty.

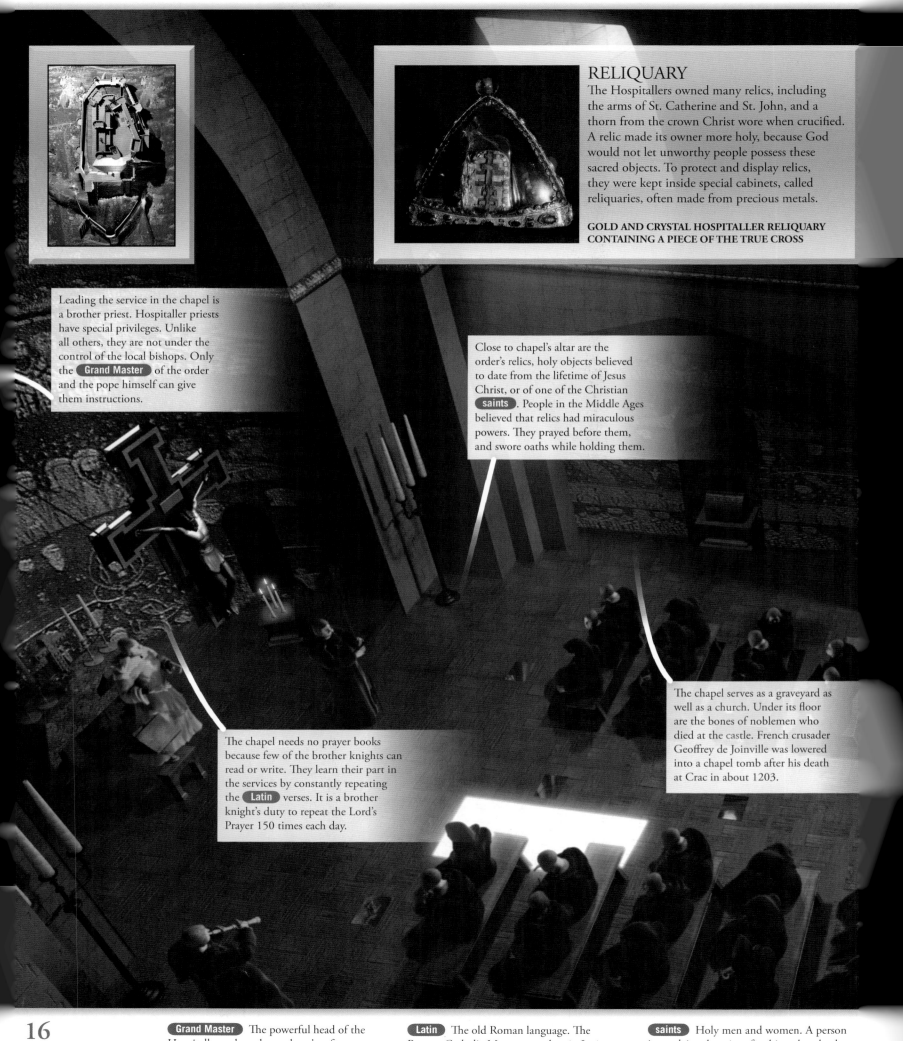

RELIQUARY

The Hospitallers owned many relics, including the arms of St. Catherine and St. John, and a thorn from the crown Christ wore when crucified. A relic made its owner more holy, because God would not let unworthy people possess these sacred objects. To protect and display relics, they were kept inside special cabinets, called reliquaries, often made from precious metals.

GOLD AND CRYSTAL HOSPITALLER RELIQUARY CONTAINING A PIECE OF THE TRUE CROSS

Leading the service in the chapel is a brother priest. Hospitaller priests have special privileges. Unlike all others, they are not under the control of the local bishops. Only the **Grand Master** of the order and the pope himself can give them instructions.

Close to chapel's altar are the order's relics, holy objects believed to date from the lifetime of Jesus Christ, or of one of the Christian **saints**. People in the Middle Ages believed that relics had miraculous powers. They prayed before them, and swore oaths while holding them.

The chapel needs no prayer books because few of the brother knights can read or write. They learn their part in the services by constantly repeating the **Latin** verses. It is a brother knight's duty to repeat the Lord's Prayer 150 times each day.

The chapel serves as a graveyard as well as a church. Under its floor are the bones of noblemen who died at the castle. French crusader Geoffrey de Joinville was lowered into a chapel tomb after his death at Crac in about 1203.

Grand Master The powerful head of the Hospitaller order, who took orders from no one but the pope.

Latin The old Roman language. The Roman Catholic Mass was spoken in Latin until 1965.

saints Holy men and women. A person is proclaimed a saint after his or her death on the evidence of miracles and saintly acts.

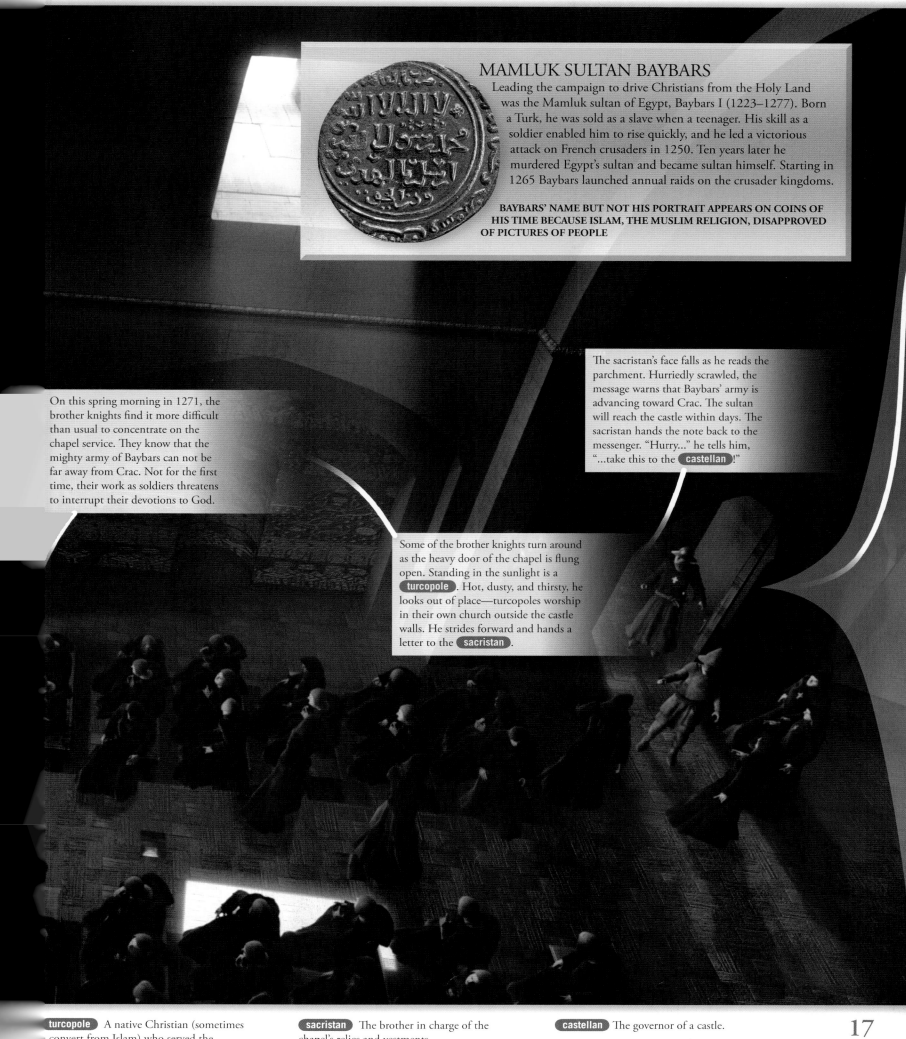

MAMLUK SULTAN BAYBARS

Leading the campaign to drive Christians from the Holy Land was the Mamluk sultan of Egypt, Baybars I (1223–1277). Born a Turk, he was sold as a slave when a teenager. His skill as a soldier enabled him to rise quickly, and he led a victorious attack on French crusaders in 1250. Ten years later he murdered Egypt's sultan and became sultan himself. Starting in 1265 Baybars launched annual raids on the crusader kingdoms.

BAYBARS' NAME BUT NOT HIS PORTRAIT APPEARS ON COINS OF HIS TIME BECAUSE ISLAM, THE MUSLIM RELIGION, DISAPPROVED OF PICTURES OF PEOPLE

The sacristan's face falls as he reads the parchment. Hurriedly scrawled, the message warns that Baybars' army is advancing toward Crac. The sultan will reach the castle within days. The sacristan hands the note back to the messenger. "Hurry..." he tells him, "...take this to the **castellan**!"

On this spring morning in 1271, the brother knights find it more difficult than usual to concentrate on the chapel service. They know that the mighty army of Baybars can not be far away from Crac. Not for the first time, their work as soldiers threatens to interrupt their devotions to God.

Some of the brother knights turn around as the heavy door of the chapel is flung open. Standing in the sunlight is a **turcopole**. Hot, dusty, and thirsty, he looks out of place—turcopoles worship in their own church outside the castle walls. He strides forward and hands a letter to the **sacristan**.

turcopole A native Christian (sometimes a convert from Islam) who served the Hospitallers in a lightly armed cavalry unit.

sacristan The brother in charge of the chapel's relics and vestments.

castellan The governor of a castle.

17

THE COURTYARD

Circled twice around with strong walls, Crac des Chevaliers is a castle within a castle. At the very heart of this `concentric` design is the courtyard: a paved open space that leads to all the main buildings. The courtyard guards access to the chapel—the most sacred part of the castle. It also leads to the Great Hall, the castle's administrative center. In peacetime the courtyard bustles with activity. In addition to knights, there are merchants, servants, pilgrims, and local Syrian Christians to be seen here. But when danger threatens, the courtyard becomes a controlling hub. Commands echo around the walls as soldiers rush to their posts.

The walls that enclose the courtyard are thick and solid. This is not just for defense. In summer, shade temperatures soar to 104°F (40°C) and the flagstones burn bare feet. The heavy masonry keeps the rooms cool by day, and stores heat to keep them snug in the cold nights.

Considering the size of Crac des Chevaliers, the courtyard is surprisingly small. A raised platform with arches beneath covers half its area. The chapel takes up more room. The space that's left feels cramped and crowded when the anxious knights spill out from the chapel.

Large halls surround the courtyard on three sides. The one on the east side was perhaps Crac's hospital. Sick and wounded knights and turcopoles regain their strength here. The knights may also nurse the sick and dying from beyond the castle walls: care of the sick is one of their duties as monks.

MUSLIM SLAVES

Some of the hardest, nastiest work at Crac is done by Muslim `slaves`. Slaves are captured in battle, or born of slave parents. Slavery is an accepted part of life: the crusaders' Muslim foe own Christian slaves, and starving crusaders have sometimes even sold their own children as slaves to buy food.

MEDIEVAL PAINTING OF MUSLIM CAPTIVES REQUESTING BAPTISM

`concentric` A circle that has the same center as another a circle. The courtyard is at the center of both encircling walls.

`slaves` Prisoner workers bought and sold as possessions. Slavery was not generally made illegal until the 1800s.

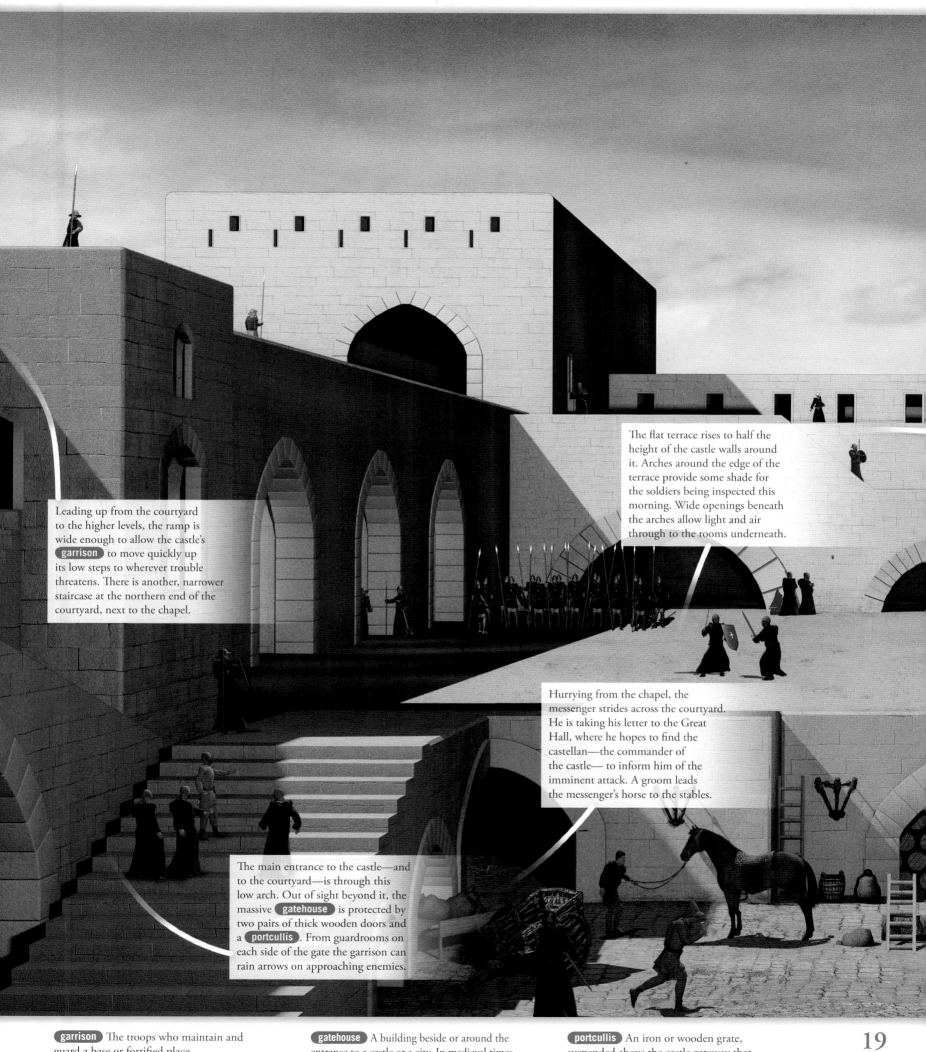

Leading up from the courtyard to the higher levels, the ramp is wide enough to allow the castle's **garrison** to move quickly up its low steps to wherever trouble threatens. There is another, narrower staircase at the northern end of the courtyard, next to the chapel.

The flat terrace rises to half the height of the castle walls around it. Arches around the edge of the terrace provide some shade for the soldiers being inspected this morning. Wide openings beneath the arches allow light and air through to the rooms underneath.

Hurrying from the chapel, the messenger strides across the courtyard. He is taking his letter to the Great Hall, where he hopes to find the castellan—the commander of the castle— to inform him of the imminent attack. A groom leads the messenger's horse to the stables.

The main entrance to the castle—and to the courtyard—is through this low arch. Out of sight beyond it, the massive **gatehouse** is protected by two pairs of thick wooden doors and a **portcullis**. From guardrooms on each side of the gate the garrison can rain arrows on approaching enemies.

garrison The troops who maintain and guard a base or fortified place.

gatehouse A building beside or around the entrance to a castle or a city. In medieval times the gatehouse was usually fortified.

portcullis An iron or wooden grate, suspended above the castle gateway that could be lowered to bar the entrance.

The wide surface of the terrace has enough space for the whole garrison to assemble. Here there's also room for troops to train, or for the staging of mystery plays on festival days. This morning, some knights are demonstrating their swords skills for the benefit of a visiting commander.

Beneath the terrace, wide columns support the low, arched roof of the armory (see pages 32–33). The thick masonry ensures that this vital building is safe even in a siege—unlike a wooden roof, it's fireproof and can withstand the heaviest of stone missiles.

The courtyard's flagstone floor has a vital function—it collects rainwater. Though little rain falls between May and September, winters are very wet. Rainwater draining from the dripping slabs runs along special channels into vast, rock-cut cisterns below the castle.

20

mystery plays Types of medieval drama that were based upon the life of Christ and performed on holy days.

cisterns Underground reservoirs for storing water. The word comes from the Latin "cisterna," meaning "underground tank."

Every part of the castle has to help in its defense, and the castellan's tower is no exception. From the round upper room a narrow **spiral staircase** rises to a **turret** on the roof. From here, the highest point in the castle, watchmen have a commanding view over the landscape to the south and west.

The castellan's apartment is spread across two floors of the southwest tower of the castle. In keeping with his high status, the rooms are comfortable and finely decorated—there's even a private lavatory. On the shady north side, a big window looks out across the courtyard.

WISE WORDS

Within the cloisters is an inscription carved upon the wall: "Have richness, have wisdom, have beauty, but beware of pride, which spoils all that it touches." The message reminds brothers that as followers of Christ they must be humble—but not necessarily poor!

Just like a monastery in the knights' French homeland, the castle has a cloister leading into the Great Hall. The cloister's open stone windows are carved as beautifully as those of a cathedral. Under the cloister's roof, brother knights can spend time outdoors, even during torrential winter rain.

spiral staircase A type of narrow, winding stone staircase found inside the towers and turrets of medieval castles.

turret A small, usually rounded tower that projects out from the wall of a castle.

CASTLE ESTATES

The castle estates contolled from the Great Hall are worked by local Christian and Muslim farmers. The knights could be generous landlords. The Muslim traveler Ibn Jubayr (1145–1217) noticed with surprise that the Franks allowed their farmers to keep half the harvest and charged them less tax than Christians farmers paid to Muslim masters.

A simple cross decorates the shields that the brother knights use in battle, but the shields of visiting crusaders that line the walls are not nearly as plain. Painted with **heraldic achievements**, the shields tell the story of a knight's ancestry.

The main entrance to the Great Hall is through the cloister that separates it from the courtyard. However, there are two other ways in. On the south side, an arch leads through from the armory, and facing the cloister is a small door from the kitchens and **refectory**.

THE GREAT HALL

Spacious, high, and beautifully decorated, the Great Hall is the castle's finest room. On special occasions this is where the knights gather to celebrate, or perhaps to share a feast. Here, too, the castellan greets important visitors from Europe. However, the hall is also a working space. It serves as a courtroom, where the knights deliver justice to the local people under their rule. When danger threatens Crac des Chevaliers, it is a center for command and control. The messenger now brings his news of the impending attack to the Great Hall, since it's here that he will most likely find the castellan, the commander of knights.

ORNATE STONEWORK

Pointed arches support the heavy stone-vaulted ceilings of the castle. It is a tribute to the skill of the medieval masons and engineers that these buildings still stand robustly even though they were erected in the 13th century. Arches allowed ceilings to be high without supporting columns. The heavier the weight pressing down upon the arch, the more secure the building.

heraldic achievements Patterns of mythical beasts and special signs unique to a knight's family.

refectory A communal dining room in a religious or academic institution.

papal legates Visiting officials bringing instructions from the pope.

As lords of the estates around the castle, the knights are in charge of law and order. At the courts held in the Great Hall, the knights respect the religion of their Muslim and Asian Christian subjects. To ensure fairness, when a Christian accuses a Muslim of a crime, only Muslims can be witnesses.

Hunting game with dogs and **falconry** are popular pastimes for wealthy knights in Europe, but for brother knights in the Holy Land these are forbidden. When the castle is not in danger some hunt gazelle anyway, forcing the order's Grand Master to remind them of the rules.

When pilgrims, kings, and **papal legates** visit Crac des Chevaliers, the Hospitallers entertain them in grand style, for the generosity of the wealthy helps them to continue their work. After visiting the castle in the Fifth Crusade, Hungary's King Andrew II (c. 1175–1235) paid for the walls to be strengthened.

As the brother knights talk about the battle to come, two of the castle's guests seated at the table strain to pick some hard facts out of the conversation. In the excitement they forget their thirst and hunger and a servant removes the dishes of food and the wine brought for them.

Bad news travels fast. When the messenger reaches the Great Hall he finds that a brother has raced ahead of him. Already the knights are gathering to discuss how to defend Crac. But the one person he is seeking—the castellan—is not here. The messenger will have to look further before he can deliver his message.

falconry The art of training falcons to return from flight to their trainer and to hunt prey.

THE KITCHEN

In a cavernous and bustling room, a small army of cooks works to feed the castle's hundreds of hungry mouths. The kitchens fill about a quarter of this household part of the castle, which wraps around the west and north sides just beneath the inner walls. The rest of the space is mostly taken up by the refectory—Crac's huge dining room—and by storage rooms. Normally piled to the roof with provisions, the storerooms are now almost empty. Their contents were used up last year, when Baybars' army overran Crac's estates and took the harvest. The shortage that followed has seriously weakened Crac's power to withstand a siege.

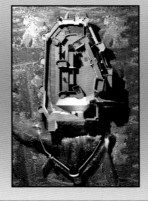

A PLACE TO SIT

The castle's `latrines` have no doors. The holes below the seats open onto the castle's outside wall. The science of germs and hygiene is still many centuries in the future, and for the flies that swarm around the stinking cubicles it's only a short flight to the kitchens next door.

In these rambling kitchens, the cooks prepare a menu that is nourishing and varied by medieval standards. The knights eat fresh pork, lamb, chicken, pigeon, and partridge. On the many days when their religion forbids them to eat meat, they have bread, fish, eggs, beans, and a wide choice of vegetables and fruit.

The servant who returns from the Great Hall next door brings the first news of Baybars' expected attack. The warning has a special importance for the cooks. They must now try to figure out how to make the castle's limited food supplies last through what could be a lengthy siege.

In addition to the pots and pans found in every kitchen, the castle has many `mortars and pestles`. Medieval cutlery does not include forks, and to make eating easier food is pounded until it has the texture of oatmeal. Knights use a slice of bread called a trencher to mop the delicious paste from their plates.

The brother in charge of the kitchen is also responsible for enforcing the order's rules at meal times. It isn't always easy. Brother knights are supposed to eat politely and silently, but not all do. At times, they have beaten the servants waiting on them and pelted them with bread and wine.

`mortars and pestles` A pestle is a club-shaped tool for grinding and pounding food in a mortar, a type of heavy bowl.

`latrines` Toilets in castles, camps, or barracks. The word comes from the Latin *lavatrina*, meaning a bath.

`spices` Aromatic substances, such as ginger, cinnamon, nutmeg, and chilli used to season and flavor food.

MEDIEVAL COOKING

Without refrigeration, fresh food spoiled quickly in the Syrian summer. Butchers slaughtered food animals just before they were needed. They made surplus meat last longer by covering it in salt, or by smoking it. Fish was preserved in the same way. Plant crops such as beans and fruit kept well when dried in the sun or pickled.

A SKILLED BUTCHER SLAUGHTERS A PIG WITH SINGLE BLOW

The baker uses a vast stone oven to bake the loaves once they have risen. To heat it, he lights a fire inside the oven. When the stones are glowing, he rakes out the ashes, then sets the loaves inside using a long-handled wooden shovel. Heating the oven uses a lot of fuel, so there's fresh bread only once or twice a week.

Boiling, roasting, and baking are the main cooking methods. Fresh meat is roasted on a **spit** in front an open fire. Keeping the meat rotating is the job of a turnspit—a small boy—or a dog running in a cage. Salted fish boils in a huge pot, and the baker uses the bread oven to cook pies and pastries.

Under the Hospitaller's rules, the knights must be given bread to eat. Though they also eat many other foods, bread still makes up a large part of their diet. Made from **rye** and wheat flour, it's like modern brown bread. The baker **kneads** the dough in a giant trough made from a hollowed-out tree trunk.

The knights are used to eating spicy food. In their native France, **spices** are costly, so cooking with them shows off wealth. In the Holy Land, the knights' food is highly spiced for other reasons. Spices are cheap here, and the Syrian cooks who staff the kitchens use them in traditional recipes.

spit A pointed rod on which meat is roasted before an open fire. The castle kitchen could roast a whole carcass on its spit.

rye The grain of the rye cereal, used for making flour for bread, and as food for livestock.

knead To work and press the dough with the hands so that it is thoroughly mixed. The dough is then left to rise.

THE BATTLE OF HATTIN

JULY 4, 1187

Saladin

The bravery and fighting skills of the Hospitallers were famous in the Holy Land, but sometimes even these qualities were not enough to make them victorious. The knights' worst defeat came in 1187 when they fought a Muslim army close to the Sea of Galilea.

Saladin in command

Commanding it was Saladin (see page 13). As sultan of Egypt, he had gradually increased his power until he ruled all the land around the Kingdom of Jerusalem. In 1185, Saladin had made a truce (an agreement not to attack) with Jerusalem, so the people of the kingdom hoped for a lasting peace with their Muslim neighbors. But after only a year, a reckless knight, Reynald of Châtillon, broke the truce. He attacked Muslim travelers passing through his land and stole their belongings.

This was enough to provoke Saladin, and he invaded the kingdom to take his revenge. The king of Jerusalem, Guy of Lusignan, raised a huge army to stop Saladin's advance. The Hospitallers joined him at the beginning of July at Sephorie, where springs supplied fresh water. In the summer heat the water was as vital as arrows and armor: without it the soldiers and their horses would soon die.

Guy of Lusignan was crowned king of Jerusalem in 1186 on the death of King Baldwin. Guy was weak and vain: everyone agreed when a knight snorted "...he won't be king for a year!"

Saladin's army was camped to the east, between the Christians and the Sea of Galilea. They, too, had water, and more troops. However, Saladin knew that the crusaders' numbers included the Hospitaller and Templar knights, who were fierce fighters, and he was concerned that he might be defeated in a direct attack.

Water weapon

Saladin guessed that thirst was his best weapon. If he could separate the Christians from their water supply, they would soon be begging for mercy—and for water. So he attacked the town of Tiberias on the Sea of Galilea. Some of the crusaders' families were trapped inside, and he

believed that the Christians would race across the waterless desert to rescue their wives and children.

When news of Saladin's attack reached Sephorie, it divided the crusaders. Some wanted to relieve the siege. But more experienced leaders saw that Saladin was laying a trap. "Let him take the town," they told King Guy. "We can always ransom the prisoners afterward."

At first Guy agreed, but Reynald of Châtillon tried to make him change his mind. Reynald argued that failing to rescue Tiberias looked like cowardice. Finally, and fatally, Guy was persuaded. On July 3, he led his army from their green camp across the parched land. The Hospitaller knights were among the last to leave, protecting the rear of the long line of soldiers.

The Hospitallers attacked

It was the worst place to be exposed to their enemy. Almost as soon as the army had set off, Muslim cavalry began attacking the column. The Hospitallers and Templars had to stop to defend themselves. To

> "A year later I crossed the battlefield, and saw the land all covered with their bones."
>
> *Ibn Al-Athir, Muslim chronicler of the crusades, on the Hattin battlefield*

The Horns of Hattin are twin volcanic peaks. The green fields around turn to dust in the summer.

avoid leaving them behind, the army ahead of them halted, too. Unable to advance or retreat, the Christians had no choice but to camp for the night in a waterless plain.

Their situation was desperate, and in the morning it got worse. Saladin's soldiers set fire to the grass around the camp—then attacked through

Saladin's cavalry picked off the knights easily when their infantry deserted them. Their horses killed, they were forced to fight on foot. Hot, heavy armor weighed them down.

the smokescreen. A Muslim writer describes how archers shot "clouds of arrows like thick swarms of locusts" at the knights. Exhausted, scorched by the sun, and gasping with thirst, the Christians made a panic-stricken charge toward the springs of Hattin—the nearest water. However, Saladin's army was waiting for them. Worn out and

frightened, the crusaders' infantry (foot soldiers) deserted. They fled up the slopes of twin hills called the Horns of Hattin. Before long the rest of the army followed them, and was quickly surrounded by Muslim troops.

Loss of the cross
The knights tried three times to escape, but most were driven back each time. They knew they had lost the battle when their foes captured the True Cross (see page 16). The knights believed that their most precious relic would protect them. Its loss seemed like the complete defeat of Christianity by Islam. Soon after, the Christians surrendered.

Saladin had King Guy and Reynald of Châtillon brought to his tent. To show his mercy, he offered Guy a cup of iced water: it was an Islamic custom to spare the lives of prisoners who had shared food or water with their captor. Guy drank, then handed the cup to Reynald. Gasping with thirst, he gulped it down. Saladin told him "Remember it was King Guy who shared his water with you. I did

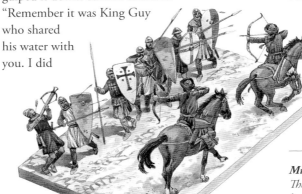

The Sea of Galilea
provided ample water for Saladin's army, which was camped close to the banks. It gave his troops a crucial advantage in the battle of Hattin.

not give it to you." Saladin then listed Reynald's crimes and treachery, including his breaking of the truce. "Kings have always acted as I have" replied Reynald, swaggering and defiant. So Saladin picked up his sword and personally beheaded Reynald.

The battle of Hattin was a catastrophe for the Christians. In their bid to defeat Saladin, they had sent almost all their military forces onto the battlefield. Only a handful had escaped death or capture. Though Saladin had lost many soldiers too, he still had a large army. With it, he recaptured Jerusalem and drove the crusaders back into a few tiny regions. It was a terrible blow, not only for the Hospitallers, but for all of western Christianity. When news reached Pope Urban III, the shock killed him.

Muslim cavalry (right in the picture) attack the column. They stood a better chance of defeating the crusaders on the battlefield than in a siege. Knowing this, Saladin lured the crusaders out of their walled cities to Hattin.

THE TOWERS

The tallest, strongest towers of Crac des Chevaliers look out to the south: the direction from which an attack is most likely to come. Towers have an important military purpose. From their **bow-loops** archers can pick off attackers who are out of reach of arrows shot from the walls. The towers are not just for warfare, though. Their upper chambers provide the castellan and other senior knights with private rooms where they sleep, work, receive visitors, and take meals. It's in his apartment in the southeast tower that the castellan learns of the threat to Crac. He rushes to the window and scans the horizon for signs of Baybars' advance.

The grandest apartment is in the southwest tower. Here the castellan has an apartment, and it's here that the Hospitallers' Grand Master stays when he visits. The tower's upper floor has a soaring vaulted ceiling. A large window faces the courtyard, but only a narrow arrow-slit looks out of the castle to the south.

The castellans of Crac don't sit in their rooms while the other knights fight. When Muslim soldiers ambushed a troop of 300 knights in 1170, one of the dead was Crac's castellan. Syria's prince Nur-ad-din recognized the castellan's face among the piles of severed heads.

Guards on the tower tops are the first to spot the approaching Muslim army. Baybars has taken Castel Blanc (White Castle) of Safita, so vigilant sentries have been gazing in that direction. Now tell-tale flashes of light to the west provide the first sign of the army's approach, as sunlight glints on weapons and armor.

From the tops of the tallest towers, guards can look right across to the Homs Gap in the south (see page 9). Less than 5 miles (8 km) away to the northeast is the crusader castle of Montferrand. It's close enough for the garrisons to exchange messages using a flaming beacon on the tower top.

HOSPITALLER SEAL

In addition to signing his name on important documents, the castellan marks them with wax into which he presses the Hospitaller seal. This shows an "oriflamme" (a sacred banner given to the early kings of France) and a hospital bed, a sign of the knights' original mission.

A private room is a privilege in the castle: most knights share dormitories. Of greater advantage to the castellan, though, is the promotion he can expect. Crac is among the crusaders' most important castles, and castellans have risen from here to the highest positions, as Masters, Marshals, or Grand Commanders of the Hospitallers.

8

bow-loops Slitlike openings in walls that are wide on the inside to allow an archer to use a bow, and narrow on the outside to protect him.

Some towers are reinforced to bear the weight of siege engines (see pages 48–49). These are used for defense as they are for attack, but only smaller machines can be mounted on the tower tops. The larger catapults need solid ground. On a tower they might shake the masonry apart.

PREPARING FOR SIEGE

Those who defended medieval castles feared sieges, for they always brought hunger and disease. To make supplies last longer defenders threw out "useless mouths"—women and children who ate but did not fight. Then they stockpiled as much food as they could find. Crac's supplies are low when the siege begins: the castle's soldiers and horses usually eat food not from the stores but brought from the surrounding estates.

A 14TH-CENTURY FRENCH MANUSCRIPT SHOWS SUPPLIES BEING DELIVERED TO A CASTLE

Like gapped teeth or rows of tombstones, the battlements that top the castle's walls provide vital protection for the soldiers on the allure. Archers shoot through the crenels between the high merlons. Wooden shutters closing off the crenels provide extra shelter during very fierce fighting.

Rooms within towers serve purposes besides defense. Some are offices for the order's scribes. Documents, weapons, and supplies fill others. The few that are used as prisons are surprisingly comfortable. When the Hospitallers hold noble captives for ransom they treat them more like house guests than criminals.

Most of the slits that pierce the castle walls are bow-loops. The loops are not always as safe as they look. Skilled archers can occasionally shoot a well-aimed arrow clean through a loop to hit an unwary guard inside.

ransom The money demanded by a prisoner's captors in return for his release.

allure A wall-walk. The passage behind the battlement wall of a castle.

crenels The low rectangular openings in a battlement wall or parapet that may sometimes be closed with shutters.

merlons The solid rectangular upright sections in a battlement wall or parapet.

THE BARRACKS

Crac's brother knights may be warriors on the battlefield, but when they are resting there's no mistaking them for anything but monks. Their sleeping quarters are plain and shared. There are no signs of luxury in the rows of straw mattresses that line the walls. And the small chests that hold their few possessions are a reminder that all have taken vows of poverty. The brothers' **dorter** is in the heart of the castle, close to the main gate. When news of the expected attack reaches the barracks, only the sick and those who were standing guard all night are still in bed. The message, shouted by a page, shakes them awake, and they rush to wash and dress.

SERGEANTS

Not all of the castle's soldiers are brother knights. Those who were not born of noble families are called brother sergeants-at-arms. Though they do almost the same jobs as brother knights, they have lower status and the two groups eat and sleep apart. Brother sergeants-at-arms wear cheaper armor and are each allowed only two horses to the knights' four, and one **esquire** (knights each have two). Sergeants-at-service are lower still. Though they are little better off than servants, they do important work as the castle's administrators.

There's no time for sleepyheads in Crac. The brothers' schedule of worship makes them rise early and stay up late. By day, the brothers are forbidden from returning to the dorter except to change their sheets. The sick may rest in bed, but if their illness lasts more than three days their beds are moved to the hospital.

Beds are uncomfortable by modern standards. Brother knights sleep on wooden **pallets** covered with straw-filled mattresses. Emptying them each year and burning the straw keeps down the numbers of bedbugs. Knights sleep in wool or linen bed clothes and are allowed three sheets.

Except when sunlight floods through the narrow loops, the dorter is a gloomy place. When night falls, the only light comes from shared lanterns. In a monastery, personal candles are forbidden luxuries, and often monks are not even allowed to sit reading near a lantern.

dorter A dormitory, or communal sleeping area.

pallets Simple low beds.

esquire The young servant and shield-bearer of a knight. Esquires often became knights themselves.

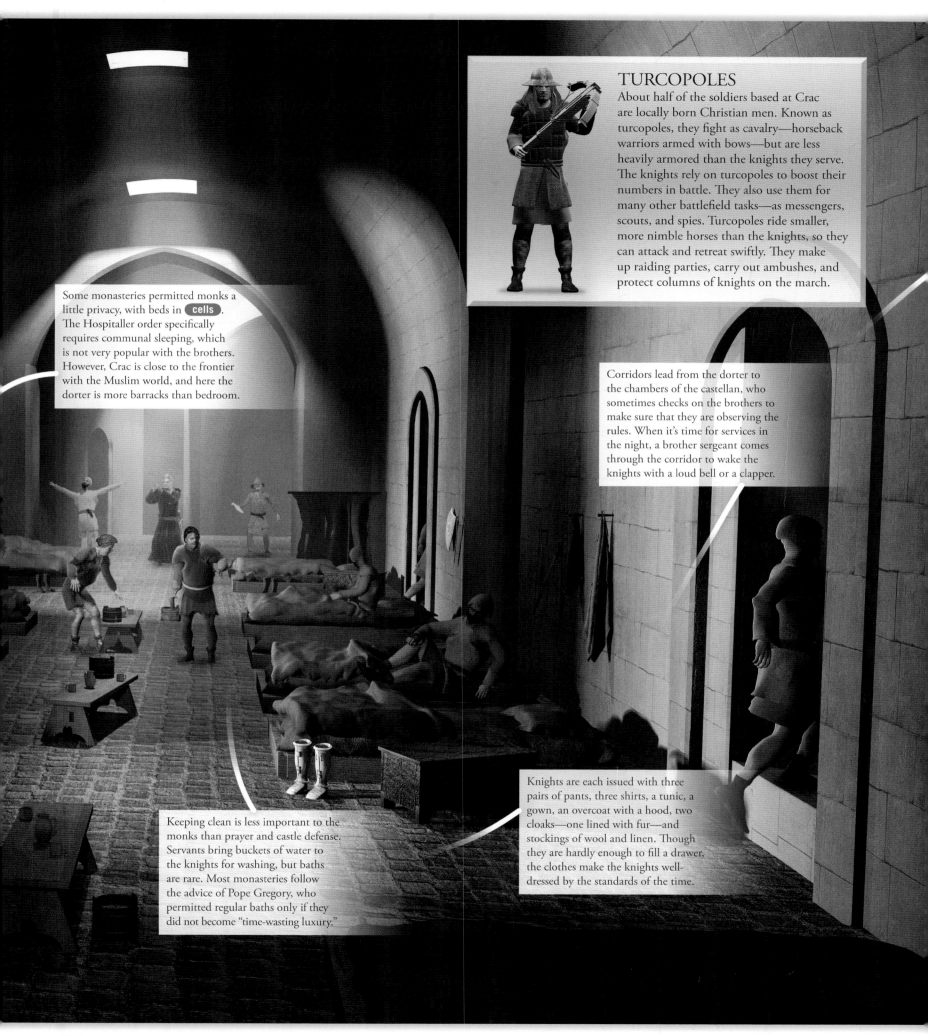

TURCOPOLES

About half of the soldiers based at Crac are locally born Christian men. Known as turcopoles, they fight as cavalry—horseback warriors armed with bows—but are less heavily armored than the knights they serve. The knights rely on turcopoles to boost their numbers in battle. They also use them for many other battlefield tasks—as messengers, scouts, and spies. Turcopoles ride smaller, more nimble horses than the knights, so they can attack and retreat swiftly. They make up raiding parties, carry out ambushes, and protect columns of knights on the march.

Some monasteries permitted monks a little privacy, with beds in **cells**. The Hospitaller order specifically requires communal sleeping, which is not very popular with the brothers. However, Crac is close to the frontier with the Muslim world, and here the dorter is more barracks than bedroom.

Corridors lead from the dorter to the chambers of the castellan, who sometimes checks on the brothers to make sure that they are observing the rules. When it's time for services in the night, a brother sergeant comes through the corridor to wake the knights with a loud bell or a clapper.

Keeping clean is less important to the monks than prayer and castle defense. Servants bring buckets of water to the knights for washing, but baths are rare. Most monasteries follow the advice of Pope Gregory, who permitted regular baths only if they did not become "time-wasting luxury."

Knights are each issued with three pairs of pants, three shirts, a tunic, a gown, an overcoat with a hood, two cloaks—one lined with fur—and stockings of wool and linen. Though they are hardly enough to fill a drawer, the clothes make the knights well-dressed by the standards of the time.

cells Small, sparsely furnished single bedrooms for a monk or a nun in a monastery.

THE ARMORY

In the darkness of Crac's armory, an ear-splitting hammering noise rattles around the walls. For it's here, in a small forge, that the castle's armorers repair the knights' helms and weapons. They clean and maintain coats of mail, too, but they don't make armor here. The Hospitallers import most of their armor and weapons from Europe, where it's made in special workshops. Though helms and mail coats line the walls, there's only just enough for all the knights, and there's constant work for the armorers, bashing out dents and riveting damaged plates. It's not all metalwork, though. Protection also comes from leather and quilted fabric.

LAYERS OF ARMOR

The four layers of protective clothing that a knight wears in battle give him almost as much protection against arrows and sword cuts as plate armor. Over his underclothes he wears a long-sleeved, quilted tunic. A thigh-length coat of mail with built-in mittens covers this. Next comes another sleeveless tunic, also quilted. And on top of it all the knight wears his hooded cape.

QUILTED TUNIC

TUNIC

HELMETS

MAIL COAT

CAPE

Knights begin arriving at the armory as news of the impending siege spreads. The armory is close to the heart of Crac, at the side of the central courtyard. Heavy stone columns support an immensely thick ceiling, protecting this essential room from attack. The stone is flameproof, too, so the armorer's forge is not a fire hazard.

Armor is costly and easily damaged by damp. To protect it, and prolong its life, armor that is not needed immediately is wrapped in greasy rags and stored in baskets or sacks in the driest part of the armory. It only needs to be cleaned and polished before use.

Barrels of sand moistened with vinegar clean mail coats. Armorers half-fill the barrels with mail coats, then roll them around. The sand removes rust from the wire links of the mail. Mail needs frequent cleaning—it rusts in winter because of rain, and in summer because the knights sweat heavily in the heat.

The Hospitallers don't wear shiny armor over the whole body. Only their heads are completely protected—by helmets made from sheet metal. The knights use wooden shields covered in leather to protect their bodies. Long straps on the back allow them to carry the shields over their shoulders when on the march.

forge A place in which metal is worked by heating and hammering, or the furnace used for heating the metal.

riveting The process of fastening pieces of metal together using short metal pins that are hammered into place.

THE BLACKSMITH

The forge at Crac is quite small, since the armorer does not actually make any weapons or armor here. A large bellows pumps air into the charcoal heaped in the hearth, raising the temperature until iron held in the flames glows red hot and becomes soft enough to bend and shape. Working (bending and hammering) metal hardens it; reheating and cooling stops the metal from becoming brittle. The hearth also hardens metal: covered in hot charcoal, a weapon absorbs **carbon**, turning the outside from soft iron to tougher steel.

The armory stores all the weapons that the knights, sergeants, and turcopoles use in battle. None of the metal parts of the weapons is made in the castle, but local craftsmen provide the wooden poles for lances, and bundles of arrows ready to be fitted with their steel tips and **feather flights**.

Cloth may not seem like much protection, but it is surprisingly effective, especially under a layer of mail. The knight's undergarments are thickly quilted, either by stuffing with rags, or by stitching together up to 30 layers of cotton or linen.

Armorers make mail coats from iron rings. They hammer each wire. These are bent into rings, which are then linked together and riveted. A single coat of mail might use 30,000 rings. Though it weighs up to 26 lbs (12 kg) the weight is spread evenly, so it does not feel this heavy.

carbon A nonmetallic element found in coal and charcoal, among other things.

feather flights The feathers attached to the end of an arrow to give it stability during flight.

CATALOG OF CRUSADER WEAPONS

Medieval warfare is an ugly, bloody, and personal business. Though arrows kill at a distance, much of the fighting is hand-to-hand combat. Knights' personal weapons are made from hardened steel and are honed sharp enough to shave with. Wielded with skill, they can kill with a single blow. Even when they merely maim, they leave deadly wounds. For without modern medical care, blood loss and infection finish the job that sword, ax, and lance began.

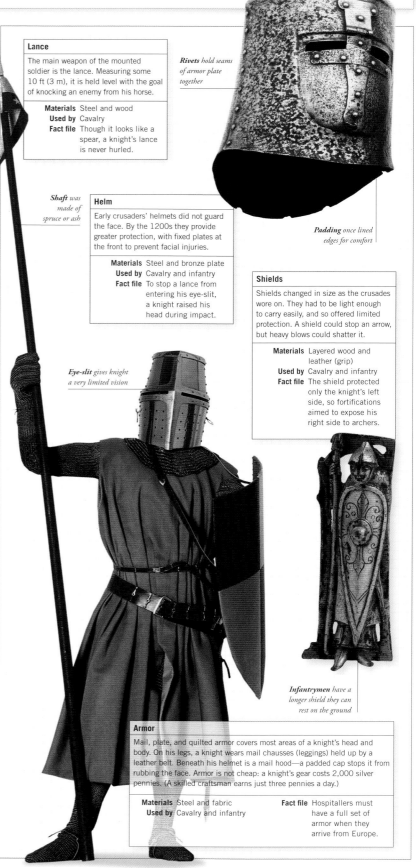

Lance
The main weapon of the mounted soldier is the lance. Measuring some 10 ft (3 m), it is held level with the goal of knocking an enemy from his horse.

Materials Steel and wood
Used by Cavalry
Fact file Though it looks like a spear, a knight's lance is never hurled.

Rivets hold seams of armor plate together

Shaft was made of spruce or ash

Helm
Early crusaders' helmets did not guard the face. By the 1200s they provide greater protection, with fixed plates at the front to prevent facial injuries.

Materials Steel and bronze plate
Used by Cavalry and infantry
Fact file To stop a lance from entering his eye-slit, a knight raised his head during impact.

Padding once lined edges for comfort

Shields
Shields changed in size as the crusades wore on. They had to be light enough to carry easily, and so offered limited protection. A shield could stop an arrow, but heavy blows could shatter it.

Materials Layered wood and leather (grip)
Used by Cavalry and infantry
Fact file The shield protected only the knight's left side, so fortifications aimed to expose his right side to archers.

Eye-slit gives knight a very limited vision

Infantrymen have a longer shield they can rest on the ground

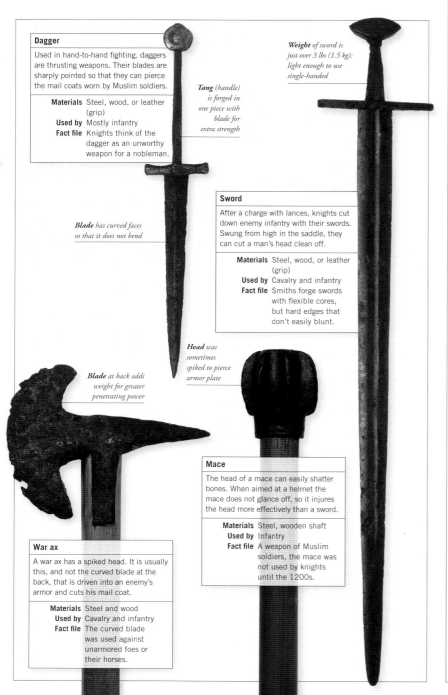

Dagger
Used in hand-to-hand fighting, daggers are thrusting weapons. Their blades are sharply pointed so that they can pierce the mail coats worn by Muslim soldiers.

Materials Steel, wood, or leather (grip)
Used by Mostly infantry
Fact file Knights think of the dagger as an unworthy weapon for a nobleman.

Tang (handle) is forged in one piece with blade for extra strength

Weight of sword is just over 3 lbs (1.5 kg): light enough to use single-handed

Blade has curved faces so that it does not bend

Sword
After a charge with lances, knights cut down enemy infantry with their swords. Swung from high in the saddle, they can cut a man's head clean off.

Materials Steel, wood, or leather (grip)
Used by Cavalry and infantry
Fact file Smiths forge swords with flexible cores, but hard edges that don't easily blunt.

Head was sometimes spiked to pierce armor plate

Blade at back adds weight for greater penetrating power

Mace
The head of a mace can easily shatter bones. When aimed at a helmet the mace does not glance off, so it injures the head more effectively than a sword.

Materials Steel, wooden shaft
Used by Infantry
Fact file A weapon of Muslim soldiers, the mace was not used by knights until the 1200s.

War ax
A war ax has a spiked head. It is usually this, and not the curved blade at the back, that is driven into an enemy's armor and cuts his mail coat.

Materials Steel and wood
Used by Cavalry and infantry
Fact file The curved blade was used against unarmored foes or their horses.

Armor
Mail, plate, and quilted armor covers most areas of a knight's head and body. On his legs, a knight wears mail chausses (leggings) held up by a leather belt. Beneath his helmet is a mail hood—a padded cap stops it from rubbing the face. Armor is not cheap: a knight's gear costs 2,000 silver pennies. (A skilled craftsman earns just three pennies a day.)

Materials Steel and fabric
Used by Cavalry and infantry

Fact file Hospitallers must have a full set of armor when they arrive from Europe.

Infantry

This 12th-century mosaic shows a knight and a Muslim in combat. Knights use their weapons skillfully in battle, but their enemy often outnumbers them. So the knights prefer to defend their kingdoms from the safety of castles, where bows are the best weapons.

Cavalry

Cavalry battles might begin with knights thundering toward each other, their lances lowered, but they quickly become messy and confused, as this image of a 13th-century clash shows. Knights cut down humble soldiers, but capture noble foe to hold for ransom.

Bodkin point

Broad point

Hollow socket holds wooden shaft securely

Arrow heads and bolts

For accurate aim each arrow must have the same weight and length. The arrow's steel head is what makes it deadly. Bodkin points concentrate all the arrow's energy into a tiny area—at short range they can pierce armor. A "V"-shaped point is more effective against unprotected enemies: its backward-facing wings do immense damage to the flesh when pulled out.

Materials Steel	**Fact file**	Even if they do not
Used by Infantry and		hit a vital organ,
mounted archers		arrows can cause
		fatal bleeding.

Crossbow

The crossbow is slow to load, but easy to master. Once an archer has pulled back the string he can take his time in picking a target. This makes crossbows ideal weapons for defending castles.

Materials Steel, cord, wood, and sinew
Used by Infantry
Fact file Pope Urban II banned crossbows as terror weapons in 1097—but still permitted their use against Muslims.

Longbow

Trained archers can shoot longbows more quickly than crossbows, but learning to use the weapon takes years. Inside Crac, the bow's size makes it difficult to use in the cramped spaces.

Materials Wood and cord
Uses Infantry and cavalry
Fact file Armed with a longbow, an archer can aim and shoot six arrows in a minute.

THE OUTER BAILEY

Between Crac's towering **bastion** and its protective outer walls lies a narrow circle of land. Though more vulnerable than the inner castle, it's still secure from casual attack. Here in the outer **bailey** the knights can train their troops, and easily reach the ramparts on the outer walls. Here, too, there's enough space to move building stone for repairs in peacetime, or the massive beams of siege engines when danger threatens. And it's here that news of Baybars' approaching army spreads as fast as the wind that whips around the Hospitaller banners flying defiantly from the bailey walls.

When the knights took over the castle there was no outer bailey. They began building the walls that enclose it at the beginning of the 13th century. At this time the inner fortifications were already very strong. By constructing the outer ring the knights aimed to make Crac **impregnable**.

The towers spaced out around the walls of Crac make it possible for the defending archers to shoot at attackers wherever they are. From the towers, the areas covered by each bow-loop overlap, so that nowhere surrounding the outer bailey is safe from archery.

The northern postern, or sally port, provides a back door in the outer walls. It was probably completed in the 1250s under the command of castellan Nicolas Lorgne. It's protected by **machicolation** and a heavy wooden portcullis slides down to block the entrance.

Twin towers on either side of the postern defend the gate against attack. Solidly built, they turn the gate into a barbican. The Franks borrowed this word from the Persian *barbār khanāh* ("house on a wall") to describe any specially strong tower.

bastion A fortified place.

bailey The outer wall of a castle. The word comes from the Old French word *baille*, meaning to enclose.

impregnable Something that is impossible to break into or capture by force.

machicolation A projecting platform at the top of a castle wall with holes through which missiles can be dropped.

The northern part of the inner castle clings to a rocky **crag**. Its hard stone foundations provide the perfect protection against **undermining**. Though tunneling through rock to destroy the wall above is not impossible, it is very slow.

Another postern gate allows the knights to move freely between the inner castle and the outer bailey. Since any gate is a weak point in a wall, the postern is heavily defended. Huge machicolation overlooks it, and the steep slope leading up to it makes the postern extremely difficult to attack.

On top of one outer tower there is a windmill. It can be turned so that its sails face into the wind. The knights use it to grind grain into bread flour and to mill food for horses. Windmills are a new invention adopted by the Europeans from the Middle East.

The open space within the outer bailey isn't really big enough for training cavalry, but there is enough space here to set up **butts**. The longbow, in particular, is difficult to master, but once trained, archers can hit a target up to 820 ft (250 m) away.

butts Archery targets.

crag A steep rugged rock or peak. Crags were strategic places to build castles.

undermining Digging beneath a wall to loosen its foundations so that the wall falls down.

BUILDING METHODS

The masons who built Crac's walls had widely varied skills. Those employed at the quarries roughly trimmed the blocks to the correct size to reduce their weight. (Moving the stone was hard work.) Once the blocks had been hauled to Crac, rough masons shaped and placed most of the stone. **Freemasons** were the most skilled: they carved the fine details around windows and chiseled decorations such as those in the Great Hall.

MEDIEVAL STONEMASON c. 1507

The western wall slopes steeply down, forming a **talus**. This makes the wall thicker at its base, forcing attackers farther out from the wall top so that they are more exposed to fire. It also provides extra protection against undermining should the enemy succeed in draining the moat.

The northwest corner tower is both the oldest and the newest in the castle. A tower stood here when Crac was still the "Castle of the Kurds." Yet this was one of the last features to be completed by the knights: in the 1250s they strengthened its gate and added massive machicolation.

Masons are always at work on Crac's walls. When the walls are not being damaged in warfare, heavy winter rains wash away stonework. Less often, earthquakes shatter the foundations. Masons cut **ashlar** for the outsides. They fill the space in between the walls with rubble.

Sections of the wall that do not stand directly on rock need extra protection against undermining. The moat behind the west wall provides this: its waters would flood any tunnel. Digging the trench for the moat was an enormous task. All the work had to be done by hand, and the spoil removed in baskets.

38

ashlar A block of trimmed stone with straight edges for use in building.

Freemasons Members of a society of skilled stonemasons who recognized each other with secret signs and passwords.

talus A castle wall that slopes outward as part of the castle's fortifications.

The south side is the most heavily defended in Crac, for this is the only place where the land does not drop away in a hill. Here the wall is especially wide. Within its thickness there is a corridor pierced with bow-loops and three strong towers.

In many castles towers interrupt the wall-walk, so that defenders can retreat in stages without surrendering the whole wall. At Crac, though, the wall-walk is continuous, because it is overlooked by the high towers of the inner castle. From there, the retreating troops can train fire on any attackers.

Overhanging, machicolated portions of the wall-walk allow defenders to direct arrows and other missiles onto attackers directly below. They never pour boiling oil, which is much too expensive. Instead, they pour furnace-hot sand or boiling water, which penetrates armor and causes horrible burns.

The ground on the western side of the castle slopes steeply into the valley, offering a natural defense. However, the knights dare not risk an attack on this side, and the walls are a massive 30 ft (9 m) high. The wall's towers are rounded to deter undermining, which is always aimed at vulnerable corners.

Crossing the wall on arches, an aqueduct brings water to the castle. The channel, which runs from a spring on a distant hill, could be cut in a siege, but wells in the castle provide enough to drink for many months.

THE STABLES

Behind the massive stonework of the castle's southern wall, the dimly lit stables are home to 60 of the knight's finest horses. When a turcopole dashes in, he blinks for a moment in the gloom before passing on his message to mobilize. Now the **grooms** must stop their routine chores, put saddles and **bridles** on all the horses, and make them ready for action. Despite the urgency, the grooms work carefully, for horses are valuable and scarce. Most are brought from Europe, and any fighting leads to heavy losses. Unprotected horses make easier, bigger, and softer targets for Muslim archers than the armored knights who ride them.

The stables form a vast vault that echoes with the whinnies of its occupants. Built from the same stone as the castle walls, the stables' arched construction gives them great strength. The few windows face out to the south. During a siege, archers will use them as bow-loops. Openings in the roof help air to circulate.

The horses stand side-by-side in stalls that line both sides of the room. Though the stables are 200 ft (60 m) long, there is only room for stalls for some 60 horses. Knights have four horses each, and turcopoles and sergeants two, so about four times as many horses are kept in the burgus and on surrounding estates.

The knights' horses are cared for by a team of grooms and veterinarians. To ensure the health of the valuable mounts, there are strict rules governing their work. Grooms must clip horses in a standard pattern. Vets nurse wounded or sick horses for six weeks, and put out to grass those that don't recover.

grooms People who clean and look after horses.

bridles The straps put around the head of a horse, which the rider uses to control the animal through the reins.

BREEDS OF HORSE

The Hospitallers use many different breeds of horses, ranging from small pack animals to large warhorses. The knights themselves ride the biggest beasts, which are usually reared in Europe. These are muscular horses bred specifically to stand up to a cavalry charge, which jolts the rider in his rigid saddle. Though smaller than a modern cart horse, they are nevertheless up to 15 hands high—5 ft (1.5 m) at the shoulder. Turcopoles, who rarely charge with couched lances, do not need such big horses. Instead, they ride faster, more agile Arab horses. The Hospitallers run stud farms on their estates and sometimes cross the larger war horses with local Arab stock.

ARAB HORSE

FRIESIAN HORSE

MULE

Horses are very particular about their food. They need to be fed grain, usually oats. They eat up to half a bushel (18 liters) a day. When the knights collect the taxes and **tithes** from farms they control, they expect some payment in oats. Horses also graze on the pastures near the castle.

Stable boys do one of the most unpleasant tasks in the castle—mucking out. Every horse in the stable produces more than 45 lbs (20 kg) of dung each day—that's more than a ton to shift every morning. It's shoveled from the stables and carted out to the fields around. There it's used as fertilizer to enrich the poor soil.

tithes Payments of one-tenth of a farmer's produce, paid to the church to support its charitable work.

SHIPPING HORSES

Horses make poor sailors. To stop them from falling and breaking their legs they must stand in canvas slings. The ships that carry them are specially built with ramps at the stern so that the horses can walk from the ship onto a beach. Since the ships must back onto the beach, they are all galleys—sailing ships only sail forward. Long sea voyages leave horses stiff and dizzy and they cannot be ridden until they have been led around to recover their strength.

A HORSE TRAVELS BY BOAT IN THIS MEDIEVAL IMAGE

The stables open out onto a courtyard next to the moat. High walls on the south and west sides protect horses and their riders from enemy fire. Here in the bright sunlight grooms finish their preparation of the horses and hand them over to the knights and sergeants who will ride them.

A young man leading a horse is one of a knight's two esquires. Like the knights they serve, esquires come from noble families and hope to become knights themselves. Esquires carry the knight's shield for him, lead his spare horses, and run errands.

Even with stirrups, knights could be knocked from their horses when their lances struck their foes. To stay mounted, they use special saddles with extra support. The front and back rise much higher than on an ordinary saddle. The **cantle** wraps around the knight's hips, supporting them.

Very few of the horses are protected by armor. Those that are wear quilted **caparisons** with **chamfrons** to protect their heads. Knights in Europe sometimes dress their horses in mail armor that provides better protection than quilting, but the weight of this soon tires the horses.

All the crusader horsemen are equipped with **stirrups**. Stirrups were a Chinese invention that reached Europe in about the 8th century. They make it much easier to keep from falling from the saddle, especially when fighting with a lance or using a bow.

caparisons Decorated coverings for a horse, especially a knight's warhorse.

chamfrons Pieces of metal or hardened leather armor to cover a horse's head.

stirrups Looplike metal foot supports hanging from either side of a horse's saddle. Stirrups give stability to the rider.

cantle The back part of a saddle that slopes upward.

On all but the shortest trips, pack animals such as mules accompany the troops. They carry weapons, food, water, and everything the men need to set up camp. Some are loaded with grain and hay to feed the horses. The pack animals will form a caravan that follows the expedition.

Mounted and armored, the cavalry urge their horses out of the courtyard toward the castle's gate. They are riding out to face a Muslim force of unknown size. Some of them will not return, but they know that if they do not stop Baybars now there will be no second chances.

Roughly half of the cavalrymen who are leaving the castle today are turcopoles. They wear light armor: just a quilted aketon, and a cone-shaped helmet. Though this affords less protection than heavy mail, it enables them to ride faster and farther as they skirmish with the enemy.

Between them, Crac's knights and sergeants have more then 500 horses, each of which needs a new set of shoes every two weeks or so. Making the shoes keeps three blacksmiths busy, and the same number of farriers fit them to the horses.

caravan A group of pack animals or wagons traveling in single file.

aketon A type of padded jacket worn for protection.

skirmish A brief clash between soldiers.

farriers People who nail shoes to horses.

43

THE RAMP

As the knights ride out, they pass through Crac's most ingenious defense—its sloping ramp. Gatehouses are the weakest point of any castle wall, so the Hospitallers have lavished special attention on this, the castle's main entrance. Completed less than 20 years ago, the ramp is cunningly designed to make a successful assault impossible. Before they even reach the ramp, attackers must cross a moat and fight their way through the outermost gatehouse. The ramp's gradient gives the advantage to the defenders, and four gates and a portcullis bar the way in. Little wonder that no Muslim army has tried to enter Crac by the front door!

Both sections of the ramp are built on a massive scale. They are wide and high enough for knights to ride two abreast. This means that the knights can leave the castle very quickly to deal with a threat—and retreat just as fast if they are outnumbered!

Through an arch facing the departing knights, infantrymen rush to join the expedition. The corridor down which they hurry leads from Crac's main gate. Like the lower part of the ramp, it slopes downward, and is overlooked by bow-loops.

Heavy doors block the route into the castle at intervals. When danger threatens, guards strengthen them with thick beams that slide into slots in the stone doorframes. Metal studs on doors aim to blunt attacking axes, and machicolation above allows the defenders to quench fires.

PORTCULLIS

Grid-shaped drop gates like these were first used by the Romans in the 3rd century BCE. The Franks call them "harrows" after the farmers' clod breakers that are a similar shape. Generally made in heavy wood, all have spiked iron tips; some are also ironclad to protect against fire. They were raised by a **winch** in a room above, where there is a quick release device. Knocking this out allows the portcullis to drop down instantly.

PORTCULLIS AT BODIAM CASTLE, ENGLAND

44   **winch** A pulley, or winding device, used to lift something up by a rope.

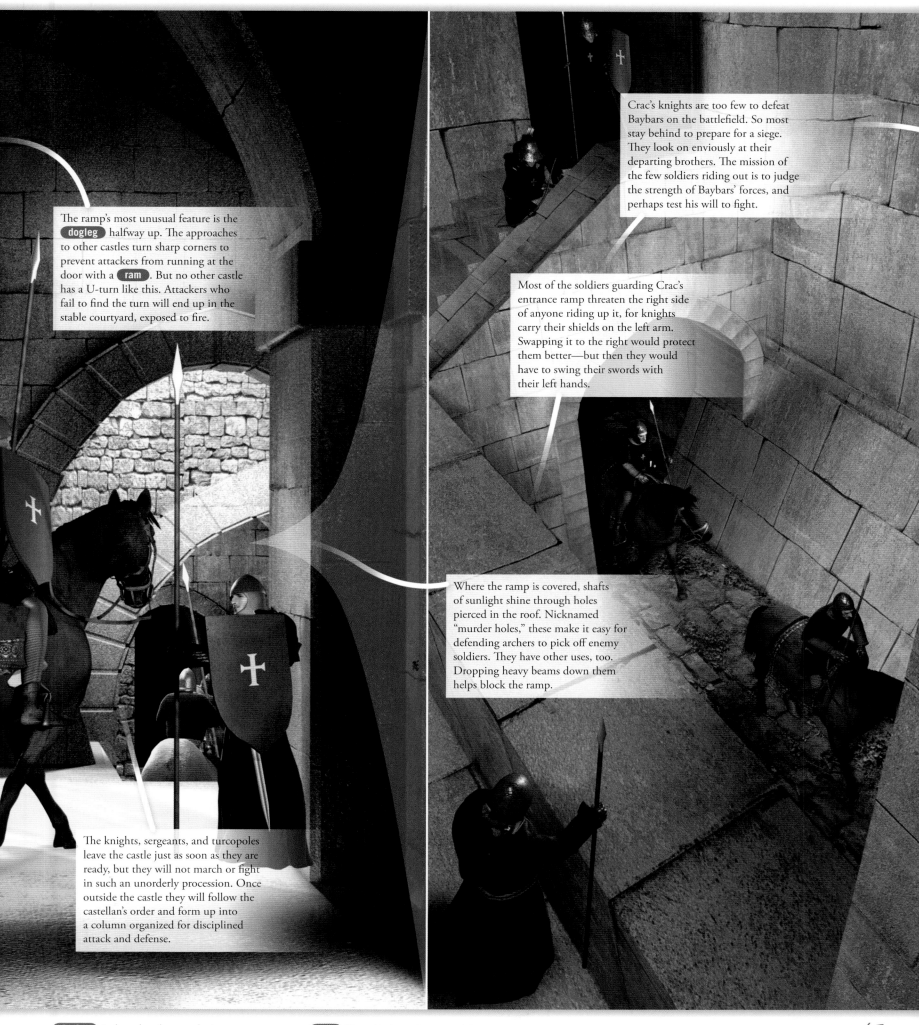

The ramp's most unusual feature is the dogleg halfway up. The approaches to other castles turn sharp corners to prevent attackers from running at the door with a ram. But no other castle has a U-turn like this. Attackers who fail to find the turn will end up in the stable courtyard, exposed to fire.

The knights, sergeants, and turcopoles leave the castle just as soon as they are ready, but they will not march or fight in such an unorderly procession. Once outside the castle they will follow the castellan's order and form up into a column organized for disciplined attack and defense.

Crac's knights are too few to defeat Baybars on the battlefield. So most stay behind to prepare for a siege. They look on enviously at their departing brothers. The mission of the few soldiers riding out is to judge the strength of Baybars' forces, and perhaps test his will to fight.

Most of the soldiers guarding Crac's entrance ramp threaten the right side of anyone riding up it, for knights carry their shields on the left arm. Swapping it to the right would protect them better—but then they would have to swing their swords with their left hands.

Where the ramp is covered, shafts of sunlight shine through holes pierced in the roof. Nicknamed "murder holes," these make it easy for defending archers to pick off enemy soldiers. They have other uses, too. Dropping heavy beams down them helps block the ramp.

dogleg A sharp bend, or angle, in the shape of a dog's leg.

ram Short for battering ram. A large wooden beam used for battering down the doors of castles.

LEAVING THE CASTLE

The knights are used to assembling swift, efficient raiding parties to attack points nearby. Indeed, this is their tactic for controlling the surrounding area and occasionally exacting tribute from villages and towns in Muslim hands. Crac is perfectly placed for this function—the knights can return to its protection and simply ignore threats of retaliation. But now there is a threat they cannot afford to ignore. The Hospitallers and their allies do not expect to defeat the much larger Mamluk army in the field, but a small scouting force can at least see their foes firsthand, so that the garrison at Crac can plan its defense.

Surrounding the castle are estates allied to the Hospitallers. Knights who manage Hospitaller estates have a duty to defend the castle in times of danger. The Hospitallers employ **mercenaries** from villages on the estates, which also supply food and horses.

Even on short journeys, the knights can't travel light. They carry their own food, supplies of weapons and armor, and take extra horses. Pack animals carry fodder for the horses. Even when there is enough grass growing to feed them, grazing is too time-consuming.

The width of the ramp and the main gate beyond means that the knights can move men and war materials out of the castle quickly. Guards on the walls above them have a panoramic view over the surrounding landscape, so they can quickly spot any threat to the knights forming up outside.

The core of the expedition is the cavalry—the soldiers on horseback. To avoid riding in their uncomfortable body armor, the knights can tie it to the saddle behind them when not actually fighting. However, they always wear their helmets and leg armor.

The knights are disciplined about the formation of raiding parties. Everyone has their place in the column: the knights lead the way, followed by sergeants. Turcopoles follow at the rear. Knights always pass around the column downwind, to avoid blowing dust in their companions' faces.

SKIRMISHING

To take advantage of the greater speed and mobility of the turcopoles, the knights usually send them on ahead in a skirmish. By raining their arrows on an enemy column, the turcopole archers can force it to come to a halt, or split it up. Then the more heavily armed knights can mount a deadly attack.

TURCOPOLES ATTACK TURKISH CAVALRY

mercenaries Hired soldiers who fight for money rather than out of loyalty or belief in a cause.

CARRIER PIGEONS

The knights probably took with them pigeons. Released with a message tied to their legs, they could fly back to Crac much faster than a messenger could ride. The knights' foe, Baybars, had an elaborate pigeon-post service: his people called the winged messengers "angels of the kings."

MEDIEVAL PIGEON MESSENGERS

We can only guess at what Crac's walled burgus (suburb) looked like because all trace of it is now hidden beneath a village. This area of housing, workshops, and offices may have been separate from the castle. But possibly its walls joined up with those of Crac.

As news of the imminent attack spreads through the burgus, local people flock past the knights' column toward the gates of Crac. Its solid walls offer a safe haven, and they fear that their sympathy for the knights will make them targets for Baybars.

Some of the turcopoles waiting to join the column will fight on foot and some on horseback. Sergeants within the knights' column will also provide infantry backup, often outnumbering cavalry. In 1233, an expedition numbered 400 cavalry to 500 infantry.

CATALOG OF MEDIEVAL SIEGE WEAPONS

Huge, powerful war machines pound the walls of medieval fortresses. Hurling rocks, flaming arrows the size of broomsticks, or even human heads, these weapons can turn a siege from a tedious waiting game into a terrifying ordeal. Called siege engines, most get their power from gravity or from energy stored in twisted fibers. Carefully aimed, they can hit the same spot on a castle wall time after time—until it falls.

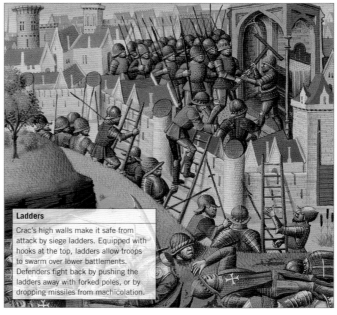

Ladders
Crac's high walls make it safe from attack by siege ladders. Equipped with hooks at the top, ladders allow troops to swarm over lower battlements. Defenders fight back by pushing the ladders away with forked poles, or by dropping missiles from machicolation.

Man-powered mangonel
The oldest rock-throwing catapult, and the easiest to build, is the mangonel. Powered by a team of soldiers tugging on ropes, it hurls rocks from a sling at the other end of its long arm. Large mangonels have dozens of pulling ropes, earning them the nickname "the long-haired ones" among their Muslim operators. Though not very powerful, they can shoot quickly and drive defenders from castle walls.

Source of power Human weight and strength	**Fact file** Carpenters can build the mangonel from trees felled at the siege site.
Missile size Small	
Accuracy Fair	

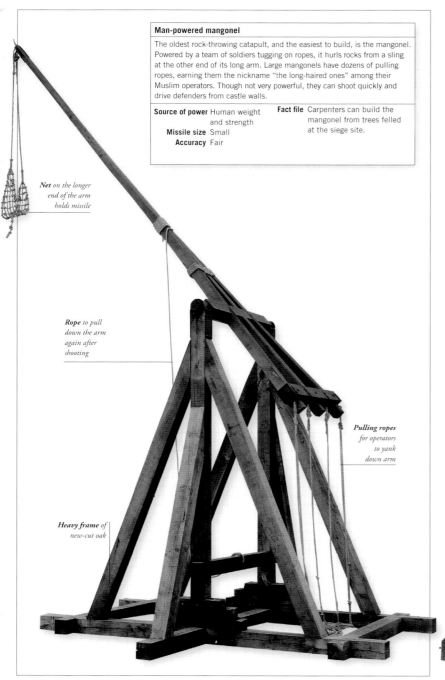

Net on the longer end of the arm holds missile

Rope to pull down the arm again after shooting

Pulling ropes for operators to yank down arm

Heavy frame of new-cut oak

Sling bag attached to a rope at the end of the beamsling

Counterweight trebuchet
Replacing the pulling ropes with a heavy weight gives these giant catapults more range. It also improves accuracy, because the long arm hurls each rock with exactly the same power as the one before. A winch pulls down the arm between shots. Called trebuchets, they were perhaps invented in the 10th century, though 200 years passed before they were in common use.

Source of power Gravity	**Fact file** The largest trebuchets hurl rotting corpses into castles to spread disease.
Missile size Large to small	
Range Long	
Accuracy Excellent	

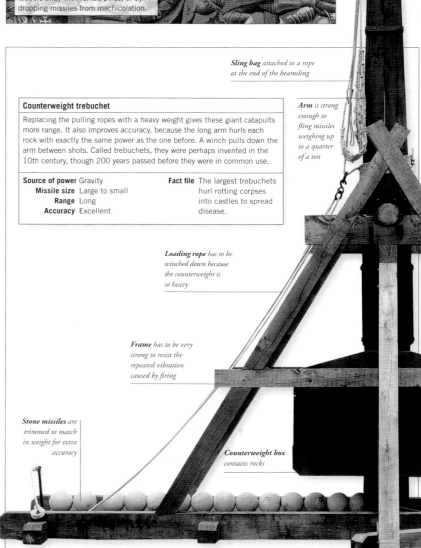

Arm is strong enough to fling missiles weighing up to a quarter of a ton

Loading rope has to be winched down because the counterweight is so heavy

Frame has to be very strong to resist the repeated vibration caused by firing

Stone missiles are trimmed to match in weight for extra accuracy

Counterweight box contains rocks

Battering ram

Not all siege engines hurl rocks. If troops can get close enough, a battering ram made from a tree trunk does as much damage as a trebuchet. The roof protects against missiles dropped from walls.

Source of power	Human strength
Missile size	–
Range	Nil
Accuracy	Excellent
Fact file	Wet hides on roof protect against fire attack.

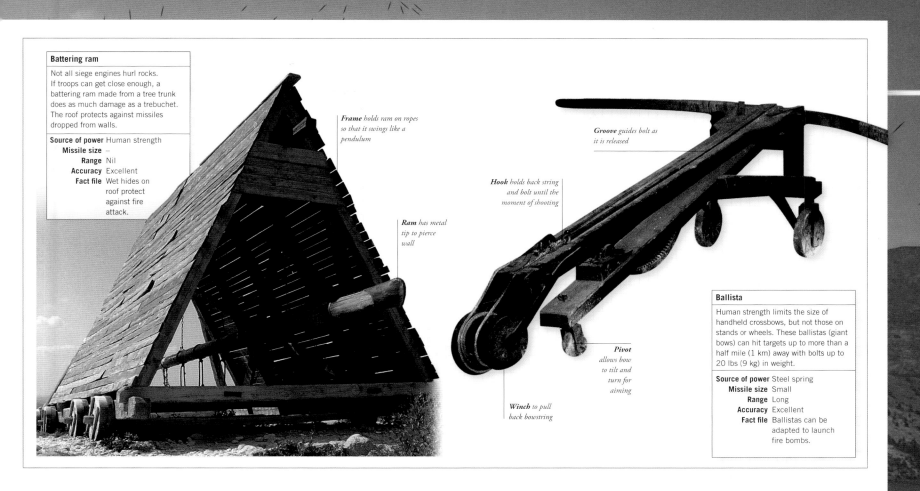

Frame holds ram on ropes so that it swings like a pendulum

Groove guides bolt as it is released

Hook holds back string and bolt until the moment of shooting

Ram has metal tip to pierce wall

Pivot allows bow to tilt and turn for aiming

Winch to pull back bowstring

Ballista

Human strength limits the size of handheld crossbows, but not those on stands or wheels. These ballistas (giant bows) can hit targets up to more than a half mile (1 km) away with bolts up to 20 lbs (9 kg) in weight.

Source of power	Steel spring
Missile size	Small
Range	Long
Accuracy	Excellent
Fact file	Ballistas can be adapted to launch fire bombs.

Torsion-powered onager

Based on a Roman weapon, the onager is named after a wild mule because of the way it kicks as it's fired. Winching down the short arm tightens up the animal-sinew spring that provides the weapon's power.

Source of power	Twisted animal sinew
Missile size	Small
Range	Moderate
Fact file	Water softened the onager's sinews, making it useless in rain.

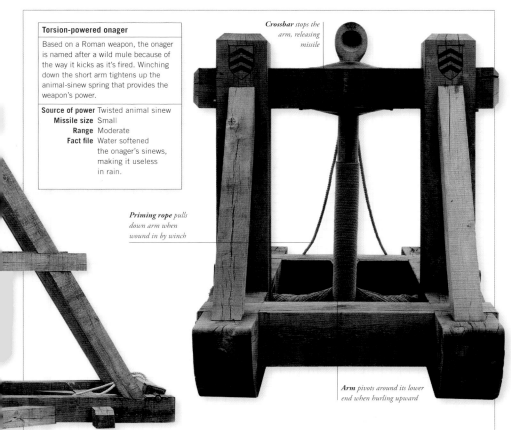

Crossbar stops the arm, releasing missile

Priming rope pulls down arm when wound in by winch

Arm pivots around its lower end when hurling upward

Siege towers

To protect soldiers scaling castle walls, some besieging armies enclose ladders inside wooden towers. A wet-hide cover protects against fire. Due to their great weight, the towers are moved on rollers, so they are useless on steeply sloping ground.

THE SIEGE

It is March 1271. The scouting party has returned to Crac with bad news. Baybars' army is vast and is carrying the parts of many siege engines. Though these enormous beams have slowed the army's progress, it has now reached the castle gates. The castellan knows that Baybars has besieged the crusader fortress of Castel Blanc (White Castle) at Safita. The town is within sight of Crac's towers, though too far away for the knights to see its defeat clearly. Fresh from this victory, Baybars' troops are clearly hoping for another. The knights are determined to disappoint them and have doubled their efforts to make their own castle secure.

Behind the barred gates of Crac, the knights received early warnings of Baybars' advance. Supplies of food from the estates to the west dried up as they fell one by one to the Muslim army. In the distance, Baybars' scouts appeared, watching Crac and counting the men on its walls.

Protected only by dirt ditches and wooden walls, the triangular **outwork** to the south of the castle is easily captured. This gives Baybars a high vantage point on which to set his siege engines and crossbowmen. From here, they can bombard the south wall.

Heavy rain following the capture of the burgus allows the knights a brief rest. But when the storms turn to showers, Baybars' engineers can be seen building mangonels behind **palisades** on the plateau to the south. By March 21 they are complete.

On Monday, March 3, the waiting game ends as the Mamluk army moves into position before the castle. Baybars wastes no time. His troops immediately attack the burgus outside the castle walls. Though the knights fight hard to defend it, the burgus falls within two days.

palisades Strong fences supported by wooden stakes driven into the ground for defense.

outwork A defense that lies outside the main defensive works, or outside the castle.

SIEGE WARFARE

The goal of a siege was to cut the castle off from all supplies of food, water, and arms. The idea was that the garrison inside would surrender or starve. In practice, a siege wasn't quite that easy. Castles hoarded food in preparation for a siege, and had their own supplies of water. At Crac there was a deep well that could not be poisoned by the enemy, and nine cisterns to collect rainwater. Hunger also affected attackers: a large besieging army had to eat, too. If a siege continued for a long time the attackers had to travel farther and farther to find food. To make a siege shorter, the attackers did more than just wait. They also used siege engines to pound the walls and dug (saps) toward the walls to that their miners could attack the foundations.

MEDIEVAL ILLUSTRATION OF SALADIN BESIEGING JERUSALEM, 1187

Baybars' position has disadvantages, too. It brings his troops within range of Crac's own siege engines. Set high on the towers, they pound the Mamluk lines. There's no shortage of missiles: the garrison collects the rocks hurled across the walls and hurl them back.

From behind their defenses, Muslim crossbowmen rain arrows on Crac's walls. Muslim archers usually use bows for attacks in the field because they can shoot them quickly while riding. For sieges they sometimes prefer crossbows, which have greater range.

(saps) Deep, narrow trenches dug to approach an enemy position so that it can be undermined.

AN ALTERNATIVE VIEW

Historians disagree about exactly where Baybars attacked the castle. Evidence comes from two sources—from **chroniclers** on both the Christian and Muslim sides who wrote about the siege, and from the archeology of Crac, which reveals which walls and towers were rebuilt after the siege. Unfortunately, there are several different ways of looking at these clues, and some experts believe that the attack came not on the east side, but here, on the castle's southwest tower.

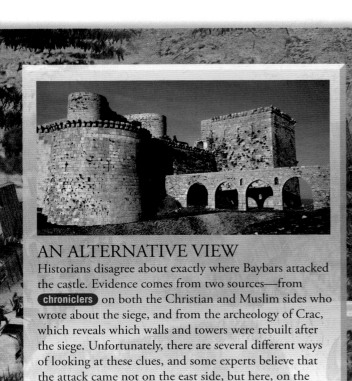

One of Baybars' first steps when he arrived at Crac was to destroy the aqueduct that channels water into the moat from springs on the hills nearby. Though the knights don't drink from the moat—it is thick with algae—it's a valuable defense. Already the water level in the moat has fallen.

SAPS

To make a castle wall collapse, the attackers tried to undermine it—by digging a mine or a sap through the ground beneath it. Arab military engineers were expert miners. They began their tunnel as close to the castle wall as they dared. As the tunnel advanced, they held up the roof with dry lumber props. Once the tunnel had reached a point directly beneath the target wall or tower, they enlarged it and filled the chamber with **tinder-dry** brushwood and often with other materials that burn well, such as animal fat. Setting this on fire burned away the wooden props, and the mine collapsed, bringing down the great weight of masonry above it.

MEDIEVAL SAPPERS USING A CAT ON WHEELS

With control of the outworks to the south, Baybars moves to the next phase of his attack: breaking through the outer walls. While his sappers are at work, they will be under constant attack from Crac's walls. So Baybars' archers now aim to clear the walls of defenders above the site of the tunnel.

chroniclers People who write down records of events.

tinder-dry Something that's as dry as tinder—the wood or grass used for lighting a fire.

When medieval writers describe "arrows raining down," they are telling the truth. When huge armies meet on the battlefield their archers just shoot as fast as they can. Arrows traveling in opposite directions darken the sky and sometimes collide in midair.

Some of the archers' crossbows are slow to load. The bow is so strong that archers must use a winch to pull back the string. To shoot more quickly, archers work in threes. While two take aim, the third winches back the string on an extra bow and loads a bolt.

From Crac's high towers, Hospitaller archers harass the Mamluk soldiers with a barrage of arrows. The castle's construction ensures that a bow-loop overlooks every part of the land around. However, some parts of the wall are more exposed than others.

To protect the sappers while they dig, the Mamluk engineers have built a "sow" or "cat" of heavy beams. This movable tunnel has a covering of wet hides to protect it against flaming debris. Under its sturdy **canopy** sappers can approach their tunnel entrance in safety.

canopy A rooflike structure that acts as a sheltered passageway.

Mining is slow and dangerous work, but Baybars' sappers are determined men. They work day and night to extend the tunnel. On March 29 it's complete. They set fire to the beams stacked inside the mine. Soon the wall above collapses into the tunnel, creating a wide gap in Crac's defenses.

Breaching the outer wall is a great achievement, but Crac's inner castle is yet undamaged. It may prove difficult to mine—the moat protects those walls that do not stand on rock. Worse, in the outer bailey the Mamluk soldiers are at the mercy of the castle's archers, who are now much closer than before.

Sensing victory, Mamluk soldiers storm through the gap with a tremendous roar—to discover that the outer bailey is filled with terrified peasants from the Hospitallers' estates. The soldiers send them back to their fields, but slaughter the few Christian soldiers they come across.

To threaten the garrison, Baybars sets up mangonels within the outer bailey. His engineers take the machines apart to carry them through the gap in the outer wall. Rebuilt inside, the engines are just yards from Crac's inner walls. At such short range, their destructive power is enormous.

THE FORGED LETTER

The pounding from Baybars' siege engines may have been enough to force the surrender of Crac. But according to legend, there was another reason why the knights surrendered. Baybars forged a letter to the castellan. Apparently from Hugues de Revel, the Grand Master of the Hospitaller order, it gave the knights of Crac permission to give up the castle and save their own lives.

GRAND MASTER HUGUES DE REVEL

After another week of siege, Baybars' assault on Crac strengthens. The knights inside are worn down by the impact of rocks hurled against the same point on the wall. Their supplies are dwindling daily. On April 8, after the wall has collapsed, they admit defeat and offer to surrender their beloved castle.

With the knights gone, Baybars takes possession of the mightiest of the crusader castles, and one that had shrugged off attacks for more than 160 years. The siege has done much damage to Crac's defenses, but in the years that follow, Baybars will repair the walls and make Crac stronger still.

The Hospitallers strike a deal with Baybars. In exchange for surrendering the castle, the Mamluk leader allows the knights to join their comrades in Tripoli on the coast without fear of attack. Baybars also agrees to spare the lives of the Syrian Christian mercenaries who have fought alongside the knights.

THE MUSLIM VIEW

FIGHTING THE FRANKS

The Church of the Holy Sepulcher was the most sacred place in Jerusalem for Christians. When Saladin recaptured the city in 1187, he placed guards at its doors to make sure that none of his troops could plunder it.

When tall, pale-skinned knights first appeared on the borders of what is now Turkey in 1096, the Muslims who lived there had no reason to fear them. They were only a few hundred armored men, followed by a ragged army of ordinary people. Cavalry from Nicaea attacked the column of "Franks," as local people called all those from northern Europe. Those who survived the attack were enslaved.

More knights arrive

But this first disorganized column was not the last. Soon, Franks were arriving in the Holy Land in great numbers. The Muslim princes were puzzled. They were used to pilgrims visiting their lands to pray at Christian shrines, and much of the local population was Christian. On the whole, they tolerated them. But these Franks were different. They were also filled with a religious enthusiasm that was warlike in its strength. Muslim leaders were too busy fighting each other to worry about the Franks. No one ruler was strong enough to control the whole region, and each kingdom jostled to control more territory. Battles, assassinations, and plots were a way of life.

Cannibals!

But by 1098, news was spreading of how the Franks had attacked Muslim-controlled towns as they advanced. Then they captured Antioch. It was bad news indeed, but it was followed by a story that horrified the whole Muslim world. At the town of Ma'arra, in what is today Syria, the Franks had cooked and eaten the bodies of those they killed! Of course, stories of horrible war crimes are often invented, but not this one. Even the Franks themselves admitted it was true. The cannibalism of Ma'arra was not

> "In Ma'arra our troops boiled pagan adults in cooking pots; they spiked children on spits and devoured them."
>
> *Frankish chronicler Radulph of Caen writing on the massacre of 1098*

The capture of Jerusalem in 1099 led Christians to rejoice. One writer called the slaughter of the city's people "a splendid judgment of God."

The massacre of 30,000 Muslim men, women, and children in Jerusalem was seen by the Franks as fair punishment because they believed that these Muslims had insulted their God.

The crusaders are seen here murdering Jerusalem's Jews. In Europe, too, the Jews were targets of the crusaders' religious hatred.

enough to unite the Muslim people against the Franks. Facing only small local pockets of resistance, their advance seemed unstoppable. Gradually it became clear that they were heading south, for Jerusalem.

The Franks take Jerusalem

They came within sight of the city on June 7, 1099. The city's rulers were not concerned. They had locked all local Christians outside the gates in case they helped the Franks to capture the city. And they had poisoned all wells outside the walls, to deny the Franks water. To begin with the Christians just walked around the walls barefoot, led by chanting priests. Only later did they start to build siege towers. When the attack came in July, Frankish soldiers swarmed over the walls from one of the towers. Once they were inside the city, they took a terrible revenge on those who had dared to defend it. It took them two days to slaughter the city's inhabitants.

Slaughter in the temples

The Muslims fled to a mosque, but the Franks broke down the doors. They rode inside, cutting down everyone until their horses

> "Christians everywhere will remember the kindness we have shown them."

Saladin, as he allows Jerusalem's Frankish Christians to leave the city with their belongings in 1187

were wading knee-deep through blood. When the city's Jews barricaded themselves in the synagogue, the Franks burned them all. Even Christians did not escape the violence. At the Church of the Holy Sepulcher the Franks tortured the Orthodox Christians who worshipped there until they led them to the hiding place of the True Cross, which had been concealed from the invaders.

Slaughter in the temples

Amazingly, even the massacre at Jerusalem did not lead immediately to a Muslim campaign against the Franks. Because the rulers of each small state hated each other, they would not fight the Franks together. And separately they could not defeat them. They followed a local proverb: "Kiss any arm you cannot break, and pray to God to break it."

Living with the enemy

Without the power to defeat the Franks, the Muslims leaders learned to live with them. They tried to understand them, too, but found this difficult. For the Franks were not very civilized. They did not wash. They were ignorant, and knew nothing of science and mathematics. They got drunk. Their physicians killed more patients than they cured.

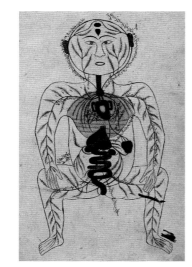

Muslim medicine was advanced. Ibn Al Nafis (1213–1288) discovered the circulation of the blood centuries before it was known in Europe.

A new leader

Divisions between the Muslims enabled the Franks to rule the Holy Land almost unchallenged for nearly 50 years. Saladin changed all this. Rising to power in Egypt, he conquered rivals in Syria and was recognized by the Muslim world as leader of the struggle against the Franks. In 1187 he advanced on Jerusalem.

The crusaders found that Muslims had left their mark on Jerusalem with many fine examples of Islamic architecture.

Saladin's capture of the holy city was almost bloodless. He allowed the Franks to leave Jerusalem unharmed. If they wished to stay, he promised they could worship freely in their churches. Not all the Muslim leaders were so merciful. When Baybars captured Antioch from the Franks in 1268, he allowed his troops to slaughter all who lived there. To Baybars, it was a fair punishment.

Muslim astronomers used astrolabes like this one to calculate stars' positions. Such devices were unknown in Europe until crusaders returned with them.

CRAC UNDER THE MUSLIMS

Now the knights have gone, Crac des Chevaliers once again becomes a Muslim stronghold. Instead of the medieval French of the Hospitallers, its corridors echo with Arabic and Turkish. The fortress has been badly damaged in the siege, and Baybars sets about rebuilding it. The work moves rapidly, even though the castle is in no immediate danger. Baybars has good reasons for wanting it complete. He plans to use the castle as a military base. The Hospitallers are still in the Holy Land, so they might prove a threat in the future. And he also wants to give the castle a Muslim identity, removing all traces of the "infidels" who occupied it.

One of the most important tasks is to convert the castle's chapel into a mosque. Baybars orders the installation of a **minbar** in which the mosque's **imam** stands to preach. The minbar can still be seen today on the south side of the chapel.

Baybars wastes no time in repairing the damage the siege has caused to the castle's walls and towers. Construction work is already under way in May 1271, a month or two after Crac fell. In October, Baybars visits the castle to inspect progress.

Later Mamluk construction work doesn't just repair war damage. Winter rains here are torrential and some 30 years after Crac fell to Baybars, a storm will wash away this section of the inner citadel wall. The governor of the castle, emir Badr al-din Bilik al Sadidi, will organize its rebuilding.

WATER WORKS

The installation of baths at Crac is not just for luxury living. Water and washing is an important part in Islamic culture. The Prophet Muhammad taught that "cleanliness is half of faith," and all Muslims wash before prayer. Bath houses also play an important part in everyday life: they are places where people meet and relax. Beyond the bath-house, running water is central in Muslim architecture. In parched desert climates, it refreshes the spirit as well as quenching the thirst.

ENTRANCE TO THE BATH HOUSE AT CRAC

minbar The pulpit of a mosque, from which the imam speaks to the worshippers.

imam A man who leads the worshippers in prayer in a mosque.

Repairs to Crac take some 18 months. In the fall of 1275, Baybars returns to inspect the new stonework. In a symbolic gesture, he calls on the emirs at his side to carry into the castle ammunition for the siege engines. Then he picks up a spade and works alongside the workers.

NEW RELIGION

One of Baybars' first acts on conquering Crac is to begin public prayers in the chapel, for Crac's new Muslim owners hold religious views that are quite as devout as those of the castle's previous Christian occupants. Muslims face Mecca when praying, and Baybars adds to the chapel a mihrab showing the direction of the holy city.

THE MINBAR PULPIT IN THE CHAPEL

When the rebuilding work on Crac is complete, the castle is once more a powerful fortress. In 1285 the Mameluk sultan of Egypt, Qalawun, uses Crac to launch a new attack on the Hospitallers at their stronghold in Margat. The city falls after a ferocious month-long siege.

Under the Hospitallers, hygiene at Crac was primitive. Though there was ample water, there were few places to wash. Baybars' architects change this, adding baths close to the moat to take advantage of the ample water supply from the aqueduct.

Most of the Muslim work on the castle repairs damage, but there is one imposing new structure. In 1285, Muslim masons complete a large square tower in the center of the south wall. Its bow-loops overlook the outworks from which Baybars launched his attack 14 years earlier.

Baybars' construction work restores the south and east sides of Crac to their former glory. These were the parts of the castle that were most severely damaged during the siege. Muslim masons also strengthen and extend the machicolation along the western wall.

A NEW INSCRIPTION

Masons working for Crac's new owners carve above the main gate an inscription celebrating the start of the castle's restoration. "Our master Sultan Baybars and his son have ordered the restoration of this blessed fortress on Tuesday 25th Sha'ban [the 8th month]...1271."

INSCRIPTION ABOVE THE MAIN GATE

emirs Muslim military commanders or governors.

mihrab The large niche in a wall at a mosque that indicates the direction of Mecca, the holy city toward which Muslims pray.

THE END FOR THE KNIGHTS

THE SEARCH FOR A MEDITERRANEAN HOME

Losing Crac des Chevaliers was a painful defeat for the Hospitallers. But this was not the last humiliation they would suffer. In the centuries that followed, they often found themselves homeless, unwelcome, and searching for a reason to exist.

Provoking the Mamluks

At first the Hospitallers did not realize how complete their defeat had been. After withdrawing to the strongholds they had left, they broke treaties they had made with Baybars and continued to raid

(left) A Hospitaller cross studded with jewels shows off the wealth of the knights. Such riches made others envious. In 1307, France's King Philip the Fair crushed the Templars to get his hands on their wealth. He accused them of heresy (denying that Christ was God), and killed many brothers.

their Muslim neighbors. Angered, the Mamluks attacked and swiftly took the last great remaining Hospitaller castle, Margat. The Hospitallers retreated again to the coastal town of Tripoli, but their stay there did not last long. Tripoli fell in 1289 as the Mamluk advance continued, shrinking the crusaders' kingdom little by little.

The beginning of the end

Two years later—and 20 years after the fall of Crac—the Mamluks were ready to crush the crusaders once and for all. A huge army encircled the city of Acre. The besieged town held out for two months, until Mamluk engineers undermined the inner citadel. The remaining crusader cities of Tyre, Sidon, Beirut, Tartus, and Athlit fell over the summer. The Holy Land was once again in Muslim hands. The defeated knights fled in galleys to the island of Cyprus. The once-proud and rich crusading orders suddenly found that their fortunes—and popularity—had reversed. Once the saviors of the Holy Land, they were now blamed for its loss.

The siege of Rhodes, 1522, ended after the citizens found notes on Ottoman arrows promising the safety of those who surrendered. Rhodes' people then urged the knights to leave.

Unwanted in Cyprus

The Hospitallers' time in Cyprus was not a happy one. They clashed with the island's king, Henry, over their power and wealth. They were accused of corruption and wasteful living. Finally, after a popular rebellion on the island, the knights realized that they were no longer welcome. They chose the nearby island of Rhodes as their next base. Rhodes

The siege of Acre, 1291, ended with the deaths of many of the besieging army as well as of the Christians within. Sappers had undermined the citadel walls, which collapsed. The Mamluk soldiers then swarmed over them.

Fort St. Angelo still guards the entrance to Malta's massive harbor. In defending Rhodes and Malta, the knights used the knowledge they had gained of building castles in Syria.

"With these conquests the whole of Palestine was now in Muslim hands. Praise be to God!"

Taqi ad-Din al Maqrizi (1364–1442) rejoices at the fall of Acre, Tyre, and Tortosa

was ruled by the Byzantine empire (the Eastern Christian Church). But with help from the pope and the kings of England and France, the knights prepared a plan to capture the island. It took them two years, but by 1309 their conquest was complete. Now the Knights Hospitallers had a new name: they became the Knights of Rhodes.

Fortifying Rhodes

The knights lost no time in shaping Rhodes to meet their needs. They turned Rhodes Town into a fortress, and at the heart of the city they built a palace for the order's Grand Master. Rhodes was in the front line of the war between Christianity and Islam, and its fortifications were twice tested by Muslim attacks in the 15th century. But in 1522 Turkey's Muslim rulers, the Ottomans, sent a fleet to conquer Rhodes. Among the 200,000 men on board were 60,000 sappers, armed with explosives. Despite being outnumbered more than 25 to 1, the knights and their allies held the island for six months. Finally, though, hunger and disease wore

Lindos, Rhodes, was one of the towns that the knights turned into a fortress to resist attacks from the Ottomans.

down Rhodes' people, and the knights surrendered. On the first day of 1523 they set sail again, first to Crete, then on to Italy.

A base in Malta

The knights spent seven years in Italy, until Spain's King Charles V gave them a new home on Malta. This small island became the base from which the Christian knights could continue to wage war on Islam. Now, though, they fought their battles not on land but at sea. They built galleys, and chained Muslim slaves to the oars. With these warships they attacked the ports of the Barbary Coast—the North African shore held by the Ottoman Empire. The Ottomans tried to end these attacks by besieging Malta in 1565, but the Hospitallers were ready for them. They had turned the island's capital, Valletta, into a fortress. Despite a siege lasting more than three months, they held the island. The Hospitallers stayed on Malta until 1798, when they were tricked into surrendering the island to Napoleon Bonaparte (1769–1821), revolutionary leader of France. Napoleon also confiscated the order's estates in France.

Queen Elizabeth II is today the head of the order of the knights of St. John. Here she is wearing the order's insignia.

The knights today

Napoleon weakened the Hospitallers, but he did not destroy them. The brothers would never again be warrior knights, so they changed their mission. They continued as a religious order, but instead of fighting Muslims, the knights took up charitable, social, and medical work. The order still exists today. Though it lacks land, it has its own government, laws, passports, and stamps, and even a place in the United Nations.

The St. John ambulance continues the original work of the Hospitaller knights in caring for the sick and injured. Here they provide first aid for a marathon runner.

CATALOG OF CASTLES

The defenses of Crac des Chevaliers were perfectly suited to medieval warfare in the Holy Land, and the castle was widely copied. But elsewhere in the world, soldiers fought with different weapons, and on a variety of battlegrounds that were not at all like Syria. The strong fortresses they built had little in common with Crac's castle-in-a-castle structure. In particular, the development of guns the century after Crac fell changed castle design for ever.

Housesteads fort

Roman soldiers built this fort in about 124 CE as one of some 15 forts that lined Hadrian's Wall. This long stone barrier defended the northern limit of Rome's empire. The soldiers stationed here fought off raids by tribes from what is now Scotland.

Buhen fort

Egypt's pharaoh Senusret III built Buhen as one of a line of mud-brick forts on the Nile River. Buhen had many advanced defenses, including a moat crossed by a drawbridge.

Location	Nubia, southern Egypt
Date	About 1860 BCE
Fact file	Egypt's forts were the first to use machicolation for defense.

Mud bricks of castle were destroyed in 1964 by the waters of a new reservoir

Mycenae citadel

The early Greek people protected their cities from warlike neighbors by building them on hilltops and surrounding them by stout walls. Mycenae was their capital.

Location	Peloponnese, Greece
Date	16th century BCE
Fact file	The stone blocks of the citadel are so big that people thought it was built by giants.

Beaumaris castle, Wales

England's king Edward I saw Crac while on the Ninth Crusade in 1272. When he returned home he built a chain of castles to control his own kingdom, copying many of its features.

Location	Wales, UK
Date	Begun 1295
Fact file	Beaumaris has a sea gate so that in a siege it could be supplied by ship.

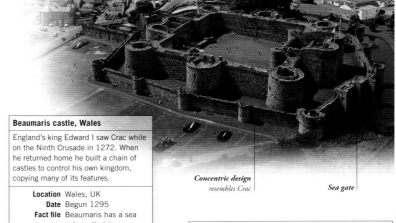

Concentric design resembles Crac

Sea gate

Sacsayhuamán fortress

Built by 20,000 workers over 80 years, Sacsayhuamán towers high about the town of Cuzco—the capital of the once-mighty Incan Empire. Its three rows of walls are built of blocks weighing as much as 330 tons.

Location	Cuzco, Peru
Date	11th or 12th century
Fact file	Cuzco's city walls formed the shape of a puma, with Sacsayhuamán fortress forming the puma's head.

Though huge, the stone blocks fit tightly together

Backward slope helps walls resist earthquakes

Matsumoto samurai castle

Chaos and violence were tearing Japan apart when Matsumoto castle was built as a fortified palace at the end of the 16th century. Nicknamed the Crow Castle after its black walls, it was once at the center of a much larger complex of walls and moats.

Pepper-pot domes top Gwalior's towers

Fort is built on a ridge 2 mile (3 km) long

Gwalior fortress, India

Clinging to a cliff nearly 300 ft (90 m) high, Gwalior is one of India's most famous fortresses. It protected a trade route north from the plains. Much fought over, it was captured in turn by Muslims, Hindus, and British forces.

Location	Northern India
Date	Originally built before 525 CE
Fact file	The castle encloses 6 palaces, 6 temples, a mosque, and 8 water reservoirs.

Vauban fortified town of Neuf-Brisach, France

Cannons could destroy any castle wall, so from the 16th century engineers aimed to keep attacking guns as far away as possible. Star-shaped designs, like this one built by French engineer Sébastian Vauban (1633–1707), provided the best defense. Triangular walls and trenches forced attackers into the open, where they could be picked off by the defenders' guns.

Location	French-German border near Switzerland	Fact file	Though described as a perfect castle, Neuf-Brisach surrendered after a heavy bombardment in 1870.
Date	1706		

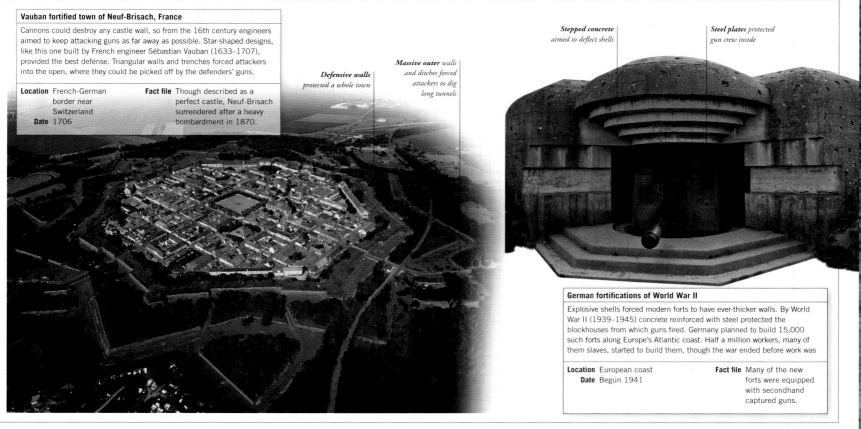

Defensive walls protected a whole town

Massive outer walls and ditches forced attackers to dig long tunnels

Stepped concrete aimed to deflect shells

Steel plates protected gun crew inside

German fortifications of World War II

Explosive shells forced modern forts to have ever-thicker walls. By World War II (1939–1945) concrete reinforced with steel protected the blockhouses from which guns fired. Germany planned to build 15,000 such forts along Europe's Atlantic coast. Half a million workers, many of them slaves, started to build them, though the war ended before work was

Location	European coast	Fact file	Many of the new forts were equipped with secondhand captured guns.
Date	Begun 1941		

INDEX

A page number in **bold** refers to the main entry for that subject

ACKNOWLEDGMENTS

Dorling Kindersley would like to thank Chris Bernstein for the index and Margaret Parrish for text Americanization.

Picture Credits
The publisher would like to thank the following for their kind permission to reproduce their photographs:

(Abbreviations key: t=top, b=below, r=right, l=left, c=center, a=above)

akg-images: 15tr; British Library 18bl; Tarek Camoisson 10br, 39br, 52tl; **Alamy Images:** Kevin Lang 59br; Geoffrey Morgan 9tr; Skyscan Photolibrary 62cr; **Ancient Art & Architecture Collection:** 49br; **The Art Archive:** 49tr; Biblioteca Capitolare, Padua/Dagli Orti 56bc; Biblioteca Nazionale Marciana Venice/Dagli Orti (A) 29tr, 42t; British Library, London 57bl; Klosterneuburg Monastery Austria/Dagli Orti 38tc; Museo Camillo Leone Vercelli/Dagli Orti 35tl; Dagli Orti 4b; Real biblioteca de lo Escorial / Dagli Orti 25tr; **Bridgeman Art Library:** Bibliothèque Nationale, Paris, France 7br, 14bl, 26b, 60tr; British Library, London, 11bl, 52bl, 56tl; Glasgow University Library, Scotland 4tl; Musée Conde, Chantilly, France/Giraudon 4tr, 5tl; Private Collection 12tr, 27cl, 56br; **British Library:** 7tr, 35tr, 51tr; **CADW:** 5b; Chris Owen: 49tl; Corbis: Archivo Iconografico, S.A. 12tl, 22tl; The Art Archive 48tc; B.S.P.I. 63tl; Fridmar Damm/Zefa 62bl; Bernd Kohlhas/Zefa 60-61b; Horacio Villalobos 63br; Roger Wood 62tl; Adam Woolfitt 60tl; **DK Images/Courtesy of the Royal Museum of Scotland, Edinburgh:** 57br; **Franck Lechenet/ Doublevue:** 63bl; **Getty Images:** Bridgeman Art Library 60bl; **Google Earth:** 8-9; **Images and Stories:** 59tr; **Museum of the Order of St. John and St. John Ambulance:** 55tr, 61bc, 61br; **NASA:** 6-7; **Peter Langer/Associated Media Group:** 24tr; **Sonia Halliday Photographs:** 58-59; **Stuart Whatling:** 21tr; **TopFoto.co.uk:** The British Library/HIP 8bl, 17tc; HIP /ARPL 12b; **Traveladventures.org:** 58bl

Jacket images: Front: **Alamy Images:** The National Trust Photolibrary (b/g); **Corbis:** John R. Jones/Papilio cr. Back: **Alamy Images:** The National Trust Photolibrary (b/g)

All other images © Dorling Kindersley
For further information see: www.dkimages.com

London, New York, Melbourne,
Munich, and Delhi

Consultant Dr. David Nicolle

For Tall Tree Ltd
Editor David John
Designer Ralph Pitchford

For DK
Senior Editor Claire Nottage
Senior Art Editor Jim Green
Managing Editor Linda Esposito
Managing Art Editor Diane Thistlethwaite
Jacket Manager Sophia M. Tampakopoulos Turner

DTP Coordinator Siu Yin Chan

Publishing Manager Andrew Macintyre
Category Publisher Laura Buller

Picture Research Sarah Hopper, Rose Horridge
Production Erica Rosen
Jacket Design Neal Cobourne
Jacket Editor Mariza O'Keeffe

Illustrators James Jordan Associates

First American edition, 2007
Published in the United States by
DK Publishing, Inc. 375 Hudson Street
New York, New York 10014

06 07 08 09 10 10 9 8 7 6 5 4 3 2 1

A Cataloging-in-Publication record for this book
is available from the Library of Congress.

ISBN 978-0-75662-838-3

Colour reproduction by Colourscan, Singapore
Printed and bound in China by Hung Hing
Discover more at
www.dk.com